HOW TO WRITE
POETRY

Also included in the Ultimate Style writing series:

ultimate style

HOW TO WRITE
POETRY

SPARK PUBLISHING

Written by Diane Mehta.

© 2006 by Spark Publishing

SparkNotes is a registered trademark of SparkNotes LLC

Spark Publishing
A Division of Barnes & Noble Publishing
120 Fifth Avenue
New York, NY 10011
www.sparknotes.com

Please submit all comments and questions or report errors to www.sparknotes.com/errors.

A full list of permission credits begins on page 177.

Library of Congress Cataloging-in-Publication Data

Mehta, Diane.
 SparkNotes ultimate style : how to write poetry / Diane Mehta.
    p. cm.
 Includes bibliographical references.
 ISBN-13: 978-1-4114-9974-4
 ISBN-10: 1-4114-9974-3
 1. Poetry—Authorship. I. Title: How to write poetry. II. Title.
 PN1059.A9.M44 2006
 808.1—dc22

                    2005037988

Printed and bound in Canada.

3 5 7 9 10 8 6 4 2

Acknowledgments

I want to thank my editor, Margo Orlando, for her thoughtful, incisive suggestions and comments, and Laurie Barnett, editorial director, for choosing me to write this book.

I'm also grateful to my sister, Nina, and to James Marcus for their careful reading and unfailing support. Thanks goes to my parents, too, for indulging my hobby, which I insisted was more important than any job. My mother taught me to have a critical eye and how to form my own opinions and stick by them. But most of all, I have to thank my husband, Tom Russell, for giving me the time to write, and for his love and encouragement.

Robert Pinsky and Derek Walcott, my terrific teachers, deserve credit for being both kind and exacting, and for teaching me how to think about poetry. Edwin Frank and Michael Morse gave me feedback and smart suggestions for this book.

A Note from SparkNotes

F. Scott Fitzgerald once said, "All good writing is swimming under water and holding your breath." Maybe this is how you feel when you face a blank computer screen: desperate, a bit scared, and unable to breathe. Not to worry. Even world-famous essayists, researchers, fiction writers, and poets feel this way every time they sit down to write. Writing isn't easy, and it takes a lot of work to write well. The good news is that writing is a skill you can *learn*.

That's where *SparkNotes Ultimate Style* comes in. We give you everything you need to know about how to write well, from thinking to planning to writing to revising. More important, we give it to you straight, in a concise, stripped-down style that tells you *exactly* what to do at every stage of the writing process. You won't find any ethereal, "writerly" advice in this book. Instead of "inspiration," we give you all the steps of the writing process, in the smarter, better, faster style you've come to rely on from SparkNotes.

SparkNotes Ultimate Style: How to Write Poetry is your key to writing great poems. We hope it gives you the confidence to write not only your first words but also your second and third and fourth . . . Your input makes us better. Let us know what you think at **www.sparknotes.com/comments**.

Contents

Getting Started

Roses are red, violets are blue ... Hickory dickory dock ... Whether you realize it or not, you've been surrounded by poetry since you were a child. Chances are, however, that if you want to *write* poetry, you're not interested in writing a nursery rhyme or a sentimental Hallmark greeting. Real poetry is different. To write a good poem, you must tap into deep feelings, observe the world closely, and put words together to create something that's uniquely yours.

In poetry, every word has weight. You can't race through a few paragraphs or chapters and get to the point later: poetry is the habit of being concise. Sometimes you don't *need* page after page or chapter after chapter to say what you want to say. Sometimes a few beautiful, well-constructed lines are more powerful than any thousand-page novel could possibly be. But just because poetry is generally short doesn't mean writing poetry is *easy*. It involves much more than sitting down and channeling your muse. You need to know the basic techniques that go into writing great poetry—and then you can make each poem your own.

Define Poetry

What exactly *is* poetry? *Merriam-Webster's Collegiate Dictionary* defines it as follows:

> **POETRY** po • e • try *n*
>
> writing that formulates a concentrated imaginative awareness
> of experience in language chosen and arranged to create a spe-
> cific emotional response through meaning, sound, and rhythm

The definition may be dense, but it contains all the essential
elements of poetry. Let's translate. Here are the key terms from
the definition that tell you exactly what poetry *is*:

- **Concentrated:** Poetry is usually concise and doesn't take up
  pages and pages.
- **Imaginative:** Poetry is not a factual report. If you do report
  on something, you must do it in an unusual or compelling
  way, with language that's carefully crafted.
- **Chosen and arranged:** You choose the words you use in a
  poem and think hard about why you use them: certain
  words may flow together better, and certain sounds may
  evoke a particular emotional response.
- **Emotional:** A poem should elicit an emotional response.
  Anyone can put lines together on a page, but few people
  can elicit an emotional response from a stranger.
- **Sound and rhythm:** The flow and music of lines and
  sentences is what makes a poem a poem.

All poems, even those that seem like complete opposites, have
these elements in common, even if they take very different
forms from one poem to the next.

**Ultimate
Style**

Learn the Styles

When you begin writing poetry, you'll probably find yourself writing short, emotional poems. This style of poetry is called **lyrical poetry**, and most poems fall into this category. When you begin reading a lot of poetry—or getting more adventurous in your own writing—you'll see that there are many other styles as well. Some popular styles of poetry include the following:

- **Allegory:** A poem in which characters represent ideas such as Death, Courage, or Innocence.

- **Apostrophe:** An address to an absent person or idea, such as Shakespeare's "O judgment! thou art fled to brutish beasts!"

- **Confessional Poetry:** Poetry whose subject is intimate or private. Much of contemporary poetry is extremely confessional.

- **Dramatic Monologue:** A poem in which the speaker delivers a speech, as though it's a one-sided conversation. Often, the speaker reveals key facts and telling details as he or she continues speaking.

- **Eclogue:** A poem about a pastoral theme, such as farming, crops, the countryside, or the idealized world of shepherds. Usually an eclogue takes the form of a dialogue. In some cases a deeper meaning is hinted at, such as our place in the universe or the human condition. Eclogues are also referred to as *bucolics*.

- **Elegy:** A mournful lament, usually written in honor of someone who has died.

- **Epic:** A long, narrative style of poem that involves heroic subjects or characters, such as Homer's *The Odyssey* or *The Iliad*.

- **Epigram:** A short, witty poem that often makes a satiric observation. It can be any length or style, as long as it's brief—the key is that the tone is sharp-tongued.

- **Epistle:** A poem written as though it's a letter from one person to another.

- **Narrative Poetry:** Poetry that tends to be long and involves a story, with characters and a plot.

- **Ode:** A lyric form used for poems recited during public events. An ode is dedicated to someone or in honor of something—a military victory, a safe return, a funeral, a birthday—or serves as praise to a friend or a god.

While you don't need to memorize all of these styles to write great poetry, knowing what shape poetry can take can open doors you may not have known existed.

Accept the Confusion

Before you can write a successful poem, you need to read
a lot of poetry. And let's face it: poetry is confusing. Even
great poems take work to understand, and not all poems
are great. Sometimes it's even hard to tell what's good and
what's not. Think of it this way: a good poem is one you click
with. Think of a song you love and memorize all the words to:
a good poem can give you the same feeling. When you hear a
poem being read out loud and feel mesmerized, or when you
read a poem that grips you, you're clicking with a poem. But
you still might not have any idea what it means.

A word to the wise: not even the most famous poets have
the meaning of a poem all mapped out when they're writing,
and they themselves may not know exactly what they mean.
However, poets are able to get the *sense* of what they feel down
on the page. Some poems have several meanings, so trust your
instincts when you read. There's no right or wrong interpreta-
tion of a poem.

Learning How to Read a Poem   To get the most out of
reading a poem, you need time and practice. When reading a
poem, you should do three things:

1. Go slowly.
2. Read the poem several times.
3. Come back to it again and again. Few people get it the first
   time.

Start by scanning the poem quickly, then reread it out loud.
This will give you a sense of the poem's sound and rhythm,
though you still might not know what it means. Don't worry:
there's no one "right" meaning hidden in the poem, out of
your reach. Understanding a poem sometimes involves simply
reacting to it emotionally, even if the meaning itself isn't clear.

Learn What You Like

The kinds of poems you write will often be similar to the kinds
of poems you like to read. Learning what you like—and, more
important, why you like it—will help you figure out what shape
your own poems might take. When you find a poem you like,
ask yourself some questions:

Ultimate Style

- Is the language beautiful?
- Are the words surprising?
- Does the rhythm grip you?
- Do the images interest you?
- Does the tone or style attract you?

If you ask yourself these questions about a lot of different poems,
soon you'll see similarities among the poems you like. These
similarities will help you figure out what kind of writing appeals
to you. For example, you might like a religious poem, even if
you're not religious, because the style is forceful and compelling.
If you pay attention to what you're reading and why you like
it, you'll be a better writer: you'll be more aware of what *you're*
writing and of how it will come across to those who read it.

Choose a Subject

Unlike an essay, a research paper, or a short story, a poem may not have an explicit subject. What you intend to write about might be very different from what you actually write down on the page—in other words, the true subject of the poem might be crystal clear only to you. A poem doesn't have to be cryptic to be great, but ambiguity and vagueness are often valuable assets.

No-nonsense poems of the "Roses are red ..." variety don't really make great art. Sometimes being *indirect* will help you write a better poem. If you're in love, write about an umbrella. If you feel sad, write about a cactus. It doesn't really matter what you want to write about, because once you're writing, it's more than likely that whatever you're *really* thinking will come out. Love will appear through the umbrella, and sadness will make itself clear through the cactus. Stating the obvious isn't poetry. Being needlessly vague isn't really poetry, either. Finding a balance takes practice.

Writing Around Your Subject   Say you've fallen in love, and you want to write a poem about it. Would your relationship be interesting to a stranger? A poem isn't a sappy card to your sweetheart—it should have wider appeal. Instead of writing about marriage directly, for example, you might write about building a house—a metaphor for the relationship. Now you have a place to start. You can begin with specific, concrete details: two-by-fours, paint, appliances, and blueprints. Describe how you build your house, especially the look and texture of the dust, oak, and hinges. Writing about the physical details of building a house is much more effective than talking conceptually about your future with your beloved.

What if you intended to write about building a beautiful house, and you instead find yourself chronicling a house-building nightmare? Don't worry: your poem may wind up saying the opposite of what you thought you wanted to say, and that's fine. At its best, writing encourages self-reflection and honesty. The more vulnerable and open you are, the better your poem will be. That's not a green light to write a lightly veiled account of your last breakup or newest heartthrob. If you love someone, it will come across in the poem without you having to say it.

Ultimate Style

Inspiration   Many people don't know exactly how they feel when they begin writing a poem, and they work on expanding a vague feeling or thought until it goes somewhere. To find something to write about, take a deeper look at the world you move through every day. Look at the objects and people, the weather, the way your body feels as you wake up in the morning. Brainstorm. Look through an encyclopedia to see what catches your eye, or turn on the TV and listen to the news. Go to a lecture on something you don't know anything about. Try to remember a place where you loved walking. But keep in mind that the real "subject" of your poem may reveal itself only when you start putting words on the page.

Start Writing

You have an idea, a feeling, and a sheet of paper or computer screen in front of you—but where do you begin? Begin at the beginning: with a thought or phrase. Some people begin with a melody that's playing in their head and try to add words to it. Others listen to a song that makes them feel emotional and then start writing. You can also simply start by describing a scene in concrete terms: "The black asphalt steamed in the midsummer sun." Another alternative is to read something you love, to get in the writing mood.

Poetry is personal, and there isn't a "right" or "wrong" way to write a poem. However, there *are* some techniques and tricks you need to know to make your poem the best it can be, such as imagery, language, rhythm, and rhyme. You need to know the rules before you can break them—and that's where this book comes in. We give you all the skills you need to write excellent poetry.

Accept Frustration

If reading poetry is frustrating, writing poetry can be doubly so. Writing is hard—but it's no harder than becoming a great baseball player, an expert mathematician, or a skilled cook. You can do it; it just takes time. Serious poets study their craft for years and write constantly. Some poets write every day. For some, writing a poem means thinking, writing, revising, and revising again, for hours and even days, weeks, or months. You might think poetry comes from inspiration, and to some extent it does—but the writing *process* is just as important, maybe even more so.

The best poetry is in some ways more difficult to write than the best prose. Learning how to write a poem is private, painstaking, and emotional. For these reasons, a good poem often eludes good poets. One poem might take you a day to write; another may take years of work before you admit defeat. The trick is to know when it's working and when to call it quits—and this knowledge comes only with time, practice, and patience.

Getting Started in Action

Ultimate Style

"October" is a very early poem by Robert Frost, one of the most successful poets in American history. You can see traces of Frost's later proficiency in certain details of this poem: the lines flow and then get suddenly abrupt, phrases are repeated, active verbs are used in interesting ways ("retard the sun"), and exclamations ("Slow, slow!") break up the pace and add excitement. Still, Frost clearly polished this poem—he didn't dash it off quickly and call it a day. He stuck to one idea and went with it.

October

O hushed October morning mild,
Thy leaves have ripened to the fall;
To-morrow's wind, if it be wild,
Should waste them all.
The crows above the forest call;
To-morrow they may form and go.
O hushed October morning mild,

Begin the hours of this day slow,

Make the day seem to us less brief.

Hearts not averse to being beguiled,

Beguile us in the way you know;

Release one leaf at break of day;

At noon release another leaf;

One from our trees, one far away;

Retard the sun with gentle mist;

Enchant the land with amethyst.

Slow, slow!

For the grapes' sake, if they were all,

Whose leaves already are burnt with frost,

Whose clustered fruit must else be lost—

For the grapes' sake along the wall.

Exercises

- Time yourself and write a poem of any length in five minutes. Once you're finished, read it out loud, then time yourself for five more minutes and write a different poem about the same subject.

- Write down the five events (past, present, or future), five places, and five people who most often occupy your thoughts. Use these lists to find a subject for your next poem.

- Write a poem about a pair of sneakers. Describe them physically, then discuss the places the sneakers have traveled, who the person wearing them has loved, or what the sneakers endure once they're lifted from the box.

Sounds

Sounds are like musical notes. They establish the feel, or texture, of your poem. Take a look at this line:

Be-bop, buh buh bo, ba-bap bap bo bee.

It's fun, casual, and a little silly. It's not serious, not with all those carbonated, popping *b* sounds. Think about the song title "Slip Sliding Away": it expresses a different emotion than the be-bop line. It's smoother and more mellow. The deep OOO sound you made as a kid when pretending to be a ghost is even more different—it's a dark, scary sound that's not used lightheartedly.

The sounds you use in your poems are musical, and music triggers emotional responses. The music of words and lines is what makes a poem a poem, rather than a haphazard group of lines. When you read poetry, pay attention to the sounds of words: how do you feel when you read them? Noticing sounds in other people's poems is a good way to start thinking about the effect sounds will have in yours. Once you start writing, you can use sounds deliberately to create the effect you want.

Repeat Vowels

Assonance is the repetition of a vowel sound: *green/weave*, *coat/remote*, *pray/away*, *fickle/tickle*. You can use assonance in a poem to be playful, distinctive, or witty. You can also use it to suggest meaning: *gowns/hand-me-downs, history/mystery, increases/ceases.* In all cases, assonance makes your poem more musical.

You can experiment with the effect of assonance by avoiding end-rhymes (when the word at the end of one line rhymes with a word at the end of another) and using assonance just *within* the line. Or you can use assonance *and* rhyme. There are no rules or limitations. In this example, from "Late Afternoon at the *Alhambra*" by Diane Mehta, assonance is used multiple times within the lines:

> The flutter of wings precedes a shadow
> fleeing over bright leaves, greenly lit
>
> with late afternoon. Sporadic breezes ruffle
> the hedge below orange trees.

The *ee* sound is repeated six times: *precedes, fleeing, leaves, greenly, breezes,* and *trees.* It propels the poem forward while tying it together through the repeated *ee* sound.

Repeat Consonants

The term *alliteration* is often used interchangeably with the term *consonance,* but they're not exactly the same thing. **Alliteration** is when consonant sounds are repeated at the beginning of words:

> The circus set up camp below the craggy cliffs.

Just because the consonants are the same doesn't mean alliteration is being used: the alliteration of *camp, craggy,* and *cliffs* does not include the word *circus,* because even though *circus* starts with a *c,* it's a soft *c,* not a hard *c* like the other words. By using alliteration, you can create a musical sound in your work and link words and sentences together melodically. But be careful: using too much alliteration can give your poem a tongue-twister effect, such as *Peter Piper picked a peck of pickled peppers.* Try not to overdo it with any one thing when you're writing. Real mastery is in being subtle, not hitting your reader over the head with your style.

Consonance is the repetition of consonant sounds at the *end* of words, such as *luck/rake, fable/foible,* and *more/mirror.* You'll find alliteration used more often than consonance, because rhymes are more typically used to match words with similar endings. (Words linked by consonance do not necessarily rhyme.) But you can mix and match sounds any way you want. Just remember that a poem with repeated sounds is generally more musical than a poem full of unconnected sounds.

Use "Living" Words

Onomatopoeia is when words such as *purr, hiss, buzz,* and *boing* actually sound like the things they represent. It works effectively in a poem because the sound creates the drama of what's happening, rather than explaining what's happening.

For example:

Low gear: the engine purred.

Purred actually sounds like an engine—it doesn't just *tell* us how the engine sounded. That's certainly better than saying "When they switched to low gear they could hear the engine." Whenever possible, you should try to use words that convey meaning through their sound, rather than just explaining what you want to say.

Choose Appropriate Sounds

Not all sounds are appropriate to every poem. Even the most creative, inventive combination of sounds will fall flat if the sounds don't fit your subject matter. Keep a close eye on the *appropriateness* of your sounds, not just on the sounds themselves.

Silly Sounds   Some sounds create silly feelings: *bulbous, butt, nincompoop, elf.* Explosive letters like *B, D, P, G,* and *F* can be ridiculous, especially when used several times in one word, or within several words. Take a look at these lines from "I Sing the Body Electric" by Walt Whitman, in which he describes a woman's body:

> Hair, bosom, hips, bend of legs, negligent falling hands all
>   diffused, mine too diffused,
> Ebb stung by the flow and flow stung by the ebb, love-flesh
>   Swelling and deliciously aching,

The description of a woman here is erotic, but Whitman also conveys the helplessness the speaker feels—the attraction is, it seems, out of his control. The helplessness one feels when one is in love can be both powerful and ridiculous. The quick succession of *b* sounds, in *bosom*, *bend*, and the two *ebbs* in the third line are explosive: when you utter them you have to bring your lips together. The repetition of *diffused* in the second line is also explosive: to say *d* sounds, your tongue flicks against the roof of your mouth. All of these sounds stop the flow of what you were saying.

Ridiculousness is the foundation of nursery rhymes, so it's no surprise that "Hickory Dickory Dock" and "Peter Piper picked a peck of pickled peppers" are made of these kinds of silly sounds.

Rough Sounds   Explosive sounds can also combine to create jarring, ugly words: *perverse, crack, gruff, jerk*. Take a look at this stanza from Percy Bysshe Shelley's "Ode to the West Wind," in which he describes leaves that have been ripped from trees:

> Yellow, and black, and pale, and hectic red,
> Pestilence-striken multitudes: O thou,
> Who chariotest to their dark wintry bed

Read it out loud, and you can almost feel the force with which the wind rips the leaves. The words *black*, *pale*, *pestilence*, and *dark* are tough, with aggressive sounds. The rhyming *red* and *bed* are rough and abrupt with their ending *d* sounds. And the tongue-twisting *pestilence* and *chariotest* add roughness and texture to the lines.

Sexy Sounds Some sounds can be sexy and mellifluous: *sleek, meander, slide, groove, surf, winding*. Here's an example from Louis MacNeice's long poem "Autumn Journal":

Whose mind is like the wind on a sea of wheat.

If you read the sentence out loud, you'll find a slight pause after the word *wind*. The vowel lingers, but it's not jarring. It would have been a much different line had he said, "The wind blows across the wheat fields": *blows* and *across* are too abrupt. MacNeice uses a lot of smooth vowel and *s* sounds, which propel the sentence forward.

Ultimate Style

Find the Perfect Word

You don't need to overstate your ideas to get them across. Sometimes a single word with the perfect sound will give the effect you want:

The slow, smooth swells crumble as they approach.

We started with the soft, flowing sounds of *slow, smooth swells*, but once we get to *crumble*, not only do the waves crumble, but the velvety tone crumbles as well. The word *crumble*, because of the hard *c*, the reverberating *r*, and the halting, breathy *bl* sounds, brings the poem to a stop. If your words physically, audibly mimic what you're trying to say, they actually back up what you're trying to convey.

Sounds in Action

If you really want to wow your audience, you can pack sounds
close together and overlap many different sounds in a poem.
Gerald Manley Hopkins was a master of creating an artillery of
sounds, as shown here in "The Windhover":

The Windhover

I caught this morning morning's minion, king-

dom of daylight's dauphin, dapple-dawn-drawn Falcon, in his

    riding

Of the rolling level underneath him steady air, and striding

High there, how he rung upon the rein of a wimpling wing

In his ecstasy! then off, off forth on swing,

As a skate's heel sweeps smooth on a bow-bend: the hurl and

    gliding

Rebuffed the big wind. My heart in hiding

Stirred for a bird —the achieve of, the mastery of the thing!

Brute beauty and valour and act, oh, air, pride, plume, here

Buckle! AND the fire that breaks from thee then, a billion

Times told lovelier, more dangerous. O my chevalier!

No wonder of it: sheer plod makes plough down sillion

Shine, and blue-bleak embers, ah my dear,

Fall, gall themselves, and gash gold-vermilion.

In the first two lines, Hopkins repeats two sounds: *m* (*morning, morning, minion*) and *d* (*kingdom, daylight's, dauphin, dapple-dawn-drawn*). It's a bit of a tongue twister, but with all that alliteration, the poem is more fun and challenging to read out loud, which makes it memorable.

Hopkins uses both assonance *and* alliteration in words like *wimpling* and *wing*. He also incorporates explosive sounds like *Buckle!* And after the graceful "As a skate's heel sweeps smooth on a bow-bend: the hurl and gliding," he follows with the abrupt "Rebuffed the big wind." The word *rebuffed* succeeds twofold: it stops the flow of sentence physically, and it literally "stops" the big wind.

Ultimate Style

Exercises

* Write a sentence using *only* nonsense words to convey what it's like to be in love.

* Write a poem about digging, using rough-and-rugged sounds that reflect what it means to get dirty, pull the earth up with your hands, use physical force, etc.

* Use assonance twice in a short poem. The assonance should involve different sounds.

Diction and Syntax

Poetry is all about choosing the best words and organizing them in a remarkable or musical way. *What* you say is important; *how* you say it is even more so. Other people might have the same idea as you, but they'll create an entirely different poem because they'll choose different words and arrange them differently. No two people have the exact same way of organizing words, and no two people have the same sense of sound.

Selecting and organizing words involves knowing about diction and syntax. Diction is word choice. Syntax is the flow and arrangement of words in sentences. Diction and syntax work together: you can't put words together without using syntax, and you won't have syntax without any words. Careful attention to both diction and syntax will help you create lively, evocative poems.

Choose the Right Word

Selecting the right word is crucial to writing a compelling poem. Remember that each word exists as part of a group of words: when choosing your words, you should be mindful of the words you've already used. Consider which word fits best into the following line:

All along the pier, the lights _____ *at sundown.*

A. lit up

B. turn on

C. ablaze

D. blaze

E. ignite

F. switch on

G. glow

H. are bright

Ultimate Style

The best fit is *ignite*. It rhymes with *lights*, and it's a strong, active verb, so it's more forceful than some of the other two-word choices. The choice *are bright* rhymes with *lights* as well, but this option doesn't really make sense. It's common sense that lights would go on at sundown, when there's no light left in the sky, so to simply say the lights are bright is not describing the action that is probably taking place here.

Try another one:

A downpour's blind beat _____ *our skin.*

A. peppers

B. smooths

C. soaks

D. infuses

E. showers

F. sprays

G. sprinkles

H. rains on

Peppers is the word that best fits in this sentence. *Soaks* and *rains on* make sense, but both are boring and don't add anything to the sentence. Most of the others aren't exactly right. *Peppers*, which has two accented syllables, follows the double beat of the previous two words, *blind beat*. Each syllable has a strong accent, made stronger by the explosive *b* sounds. The *p* in *peppers* is similarly explosive. Plus, if you use the word *peppers*, you can almost feel that beat on your skin.

To figure out which word to choose in your poem, you should consider a lot of possibilities, just as we did here. You can consult a thesaurus or rhyming dictionary for words that have similar sounds and try to narrow down the most suitable words. Sometimes it takes trial and error: put a word in, take it out, try a different word, and so on, until you discover the word that feels right. As you experiment, you may find that the sentence itself isn't working. You might decide to scrap the sentence and switch directions. Deleting words and sentences and adding others is how strong, vivid poems get written.

Create New Words

In the German language, if you don't have the right word, you create it by joining two existing words, such as *krankenhaus*: this is the word for *hospital*, but it literally means "sick house." In poetry, you can do the same thing. The following lines from "Ode to Psyche" by Keats offer excellent examples of word creations:

> Far, far around shall those dark-clustered trees
> Fledge the wild-ridged mountains steep by steep;

Both *dark-clustered* and *wild-ridged* give you a more immediate and thrilling sense of the scene than you'd get if Keats had simply described it with a lot more words. The word choice is also smart—it wouldn't be as powerful if he'd said *dark-leafed* because then you wouldn't know that the trees were clustered together.

Use Your Thesaurus

The thesaurus is a terrific tool. However, avoid simply seeking out big, unusual words—these won't impress anyone. Words have to come to the poem naturally, and if you insert a word that you feel awkward using in daily speech, it'll probably sound awkward in the poem. Instead of using the thesaurus to find words you've never heard before, try using it to find synonyms for words that don't fit smoothly into your poem. You might need a two-syllable word rather than a one-syllable word, or a word that starts with S rather than T. By perusing your thesaurus, you might find a word that's slightly more accurate, one that perfectly complements what's already in the poem.

Ultimate Style

You can also use your thesaurus to find antonyms, or opposites, for a word. Even if you think you know what you want to say, you should still consider taking a look at antonyms. You might be surprised to realize that you actually mean the opposite of what you thought you wanted to say. Without the thesaurus, you might have overlooked that possibility completely.

Spice Up Your Syntax

You should strive to make your syntax (arrangement of words) as exciting as possible. Exciting syntax is rhythmic—lines have punch and a sense of movement. The words seem to jump off the page. Exciting syntax isn't only for "exciting" poems—even those that are melancholy, pensive, or mournful need syntax that makes the ideas come alive. Avoiding careful syntax is a way of avoiding writing poetry. Without turns of phrases, adept constructions, and strategic placement of sounds, you don't have a poem—you have prose with line breaks.

Dull syntax is plodding, boring, and flat. Readers will lose interest in what you're saying, and your ideas won't soar. To determine whether your syntax needs some spicing up, consider these questions:

- Are the sentences full of passive verbs? Passive verbs are verbs that use a form of "to be" plus the past participle of a verb: *are given, is seen, were killed*. These are less vivid than active verbs—*give, see, kill*.
- Are your words arranged in the standard subject-verb-object form? "The man eats apples," "The girl raises birds," and "The boy kills ants" are all sentences that use the subject-verb-object arrangement. Too many of these types of sentences can make your poem boring.
- Are your poem's lines so balanced that they sound like nursery rhymes? You don't want a singsong syntax when you're writing more serious poems.

Take a look at these two examples. Both are essentially the same poem—but one has strong, lively syntax and the other does not:

A
Sounds of real life
hooked in their corner of time
rewind, a sea squall miles out
unseasonably rages.

B

Sounds of real life rewind,
they are hooked in their corner of time.
A sea squall rages unseasonably,
miles out.

Version A is much better than version B, even though the words are almost the same. Version B sounds like prose, and it gives you everything up front: you find out that the "sounds of real life rewind" immediately, rather than a few seconds later. In version A, you first find out that the "sounds of real life" are hooked in their corner of time; *then* you get to the real-life action, "rewind," which has more force when it ends the line. The same goes for the sea squall that, we discover, "unseasonably rages."

If we say, as in version B, that the sea squall rages, it sounds okay at first. But then you read on and "miles out" just hangs there and seems unnecessary. By delaying the violent action of *rages* until the end, and further delaying it with the

word *unseasonably*, the word *rages* has much more oomph.
Not only does it rage, it rages *unseasonably*. The careful syntax
makes these lines come alive.

Ending with a Verb   A good way to spice up your syntax is
to end a line with a verb. Here's an example of a sentence that
ends powerfully with a verb:

> All things function in tandem,
> even the pavement against which rain ricochets.

You can see the rain ricochet off the pavement, because there's
only blank space there and nothing to distract your attention
from the action. Since the line ends with a verb, the action
continues. You can still feel the rain ricocheting after that
sentence ends.

Syncopate Your Phrases

In music, **syncopation** is a pattern that is temporarily suspended,
usually by stressing the weak beat. Think of the well-known
Scott Joplin song for piano, "The Entertainer": the rhythm
in this song is syncopated. In poetry, think of syncopation as
a surprise. You're reading along, then suddenly you stumble:
the words and pauses pile up in no particular order. Then you
resume the flow, abbreviate it, and resume again.

Syncopation is a way of making your syntax unexpected
and interesting. Take a look at the syncopation in the first
stanza of "God's Grandeur" by Gerald Manley Hopkins:

> The world is charged with the grandeur of God.
> It will flame out, like shining from shook foil;
> It gathers to a greatness, like the ooze of oil
> Crushed. Why do men then now not reck his rod?
> Generations have trod, have trod, have trod;
> And all is seared with trade; bleared, smeared with toil;
> And wears man's smudge and shares man's smell: the soil
> Is bare now, nor can foot feel, being shod.

The poem is full of interruptions—it doesn't flow smoothly. Hopkins uses many semicolons and punctuation at the ends of lines, breaking up the lines and forcing us to pause. He also breaks sentences unexpectedly, such as breaking up "It gathers to a greatness, like the ooze of oil / Crushed." *Crushed* is startling, and it seems to halt the line before it even begins. The words Hopkins uses are musical, linked by assonance, consonance, and alliteration: *shining/shook, gathers/greatness, ooze/oil, reck/rod, smudge/shares/smell/soil, foot/feel*. He uses internal rhymes with *seared/bleared/smeared*. All of this makes Hopkins's syntax lively and arresting.

Look Before and After

Be aware of what comes before and after each line, since the surrounding lines often have an impact on the effect of the syntax. Lines don't exist independently—they work together to create the poem. Think of it as running a marathon. You start out with a bang, then pace yourself, then give it all you can. The pace varies. Think of your arms and legs as syntax.

Sometimes they move forcefully, pumping to help you go faster, and other times they remain mellow and loose, keeping you going at a consistent, but not aggressive, pace. It's the same thing, from line to line, with poetry. You need to vary the sounds, speed, and line length to make it interesting and to get you to a good finish.

Be Emotional

Diction and syntax work together to create emotion, making your poem sound sexy, mellow, or agitated, just to name a few possibilities. That doesn't mean you're necessarily writing about something sexy, mellow, or agitating. It means that the words themselves, and how they're used in lines and sentences, have their *own* meaning. Here's a nonsense poem with words that emote sexiness:

> Sirens, scintillating verbs, grow grizzly afterwards,
> After the raving references, the slow, substantial lacework
> Soulful, siphoning crazy, and axed with fire.

The words pop aggressively and move forward forcefully, and there are no harsh, abrupt sounds or pauses to keep the line from moving ahead. The opposite effect can be created by using very simple, down-to-earth syntax:

> Sirens and their verbs grow,
> and after the references of lacework
> are crazy, axed with fire.

Here's the same idea, but more agitated:

> Sirens, verbs scintillate,
> grow grizzly–
> no! raving lacework crazily
> axed with fire–

The words, regardless of what they mean, react to the way they're used in lines and sentences. The best poems convey emotions through the way they're written and the sounds they use, not through what's actually being said.

Ultimate Style

Use Simple Syntax

Complex, zingy syntax isn't everything. Plenty of people write more simply, with syntax that doesn't detract from heady ideas. You should always strive to make your poems lively, and you shouldn't discount simple syntax as a tool that can help you do so. Take a look at Emily Dickinson's poem 1092:

> It was not Saint – it was too large –
> Nor Snow – it was too small –
> It only held itself aloof
> Like something spiritual –

Her syntax is straightforward, and the poem seems very simple. But her words, while not descriptive and edgy, convey something much greater and unresolved. Dickinson can be sharper in her syntax, but here, as in many poems, she writes in a circle:

she sets up a situation or argument and closes it (sometimes by keeping it open). The ideas behind the words are almost like riddles, and we don't know exactly what she means. Her simple syntax is like an egg, through which ideas burst.

Diction and Syntax in Action

Take a look at "Clearances, #8" by Seamus Heaney, in which Heaney masters diction and syntax in a number of ways.

Clearances, #8

I thought of walking round and round a space
Utterly empty, utterly a source
Where the decked chestnut tree had lost its place
In our front hedge above the wallflowers.
The white chips jumped and jumped and skited high.
I heard the hatchet's differentiated
Accurate cut, the crack, the sigh
And collapse of what luxuriated
Through the shocked tips and wreckage of it all.
Deep planted and long gone, my coeval
Chestnut from a jam jar in a hole,
Its heft and hush become a bright nowhere,
A soul ramifying and forever
Silent, beyond silence listened for.

Heaney varies the length of his sentences by including two four-line sentences, a one-line sentence, and a five-line sentence. The pace varies too. He starts off at a regular pace, speeds up at "utterly empty, utterly a source," and uses repetition to emphasize the hand-wringing implied. In the middle of the poem he rhymes *hatchet* and *accurate*, then puts three words with sharp C sounds next to each other: *accurate, cut, crack*. The tone of the poem, through the sudden, sharp sounds and stop-and-go rhythm, transforms and becomes tense and agitated. *Differentiated* and *luxuriated* match up, and then he slows down with two monosyllabic words, "shocked tips."

After speeding up again in the last part of the poem, he ends slowly, with a kind of openness, also matching up *forever* with *for*. Note that he pulls back, brilliantly, right at the last sentence, by pausing after *silent*, which, by stopping the flow, *creates* a silence. Then he lets go, and with "listened for," leaves the sentence hanging.

Ultimate Style

Exercises

*   Write a five-line poem, then go back and change one word in every line, trying to make your poem better.

*   Create ten original adjectives by combining two words. Then write a short poem using at least two of them.

*   Take a look at a poem you've written (or, if you don't have one, write one!). Figure out where you can change the syntax to create a more lively poem. Try ending lines with verbs, improving word choice, syncopating your phrases, and adding more emotion to the lines.

Figurative Language

In general, poems are short—you need to pack a lot into a small space. Poems are also evocative and emotional, and the feelings they elicit in readers are just as important as what the poems are actually about. To make your poem effective, you need to do more than just write what you mean. You need to consider the vividness of your language and images in order to create the world of the poem.

When you use language in a nonliteral way, you're using a figure of speech. Figures of speech can include similes, metaphors, hyperbole, and personification, just to name a few. When you create such an expression, you're using figurative language—language that is used creatively, not just literally. Figurative language can make your poem unique, exciting, and memorable, and it's a way to get vivid, concrete images into your poem. When you learn to use figurative language well, you can make your poetry soar.

4

Use "Like" or "As"

A simile is a comparison using the words *like* or *as*. A simile is an *explicit* comparison—readers don't have to guess what you're saying. It creates a specific, vivid image and can make readers see something in a new way. Take a look at this example from "Midsummer" by Derek Walcott:

The jet bores like a silverfish through volumes of cloud–

The simile appears right up front—"The jet bores *like* a silverfish"—and it gives us a clear image of what's happening. We can see the slim, silvery jet moving fast. It's a lot more compelling a beginning than if he just said, "The jet bores through volumes of cloud." The simile gives you a second image: we see the jet boring through clouds, plus a silverfish swimming underwater.

When you use a simile, be sure that your comparison makes sense. If Walcott had said "The jet bores like a flower," readers would have no idea what he was talking about—the second image, the flower, doesn't make sense. It doesn't explain the movement of a jet in a sensible way. Originality is always vital to a poem, but if you make an unusual comparison just for the sake of being *different*, your poem will suffer.

Ultimate Style

Comparing Carefully   You should compare things deliberately and carefully. If you want to compare a first kiss to an airplane taking off, fine; you might also compare it to an explosion, a punch, or even a wilting flower. Whatever you choose, make sure your comparison is appropriate to your subject matter. If you're writing a love poem and compare a first kiss to a punch, you're suggesting violence and shock along with love. Likewise, if you compare that first kiss to a wilting flower, you won't be writing about love at all—your poem will suggest disappointment instead. Just because the image is pretty or unusual doesn't mean it's right for your poem.

Use Metaphors

A metaphor is a comparison that doesn't use *like* or *as*. If you say "You're an ogre" or "You're a saint," you've created a metaphor. As with a simile, you use a metaphor to make a comparison, but this time the comparison is *implicit*. By saying something *is* something else, you're *implying* they're similar. This can actually be a more powerful type of comparison than a simile, since you're actually equating two things: you're not just *like* a saint, you *are* a saint. Shakespeare gave us our most famous example of a metaphor:

> All the world's a stage.

Shakespeare compares earth to a stage without actually saying "The world is like a stage." The comparison is implicit, not explicit, and it's a powerful image.

An entire poem by Emily Dickinson, poem 825, is made up of a very concise metaphor:

> An Hour is a Sea
> Between a few, and me –
> With them would Harbor be –

She's comparing an abstract concept, an hour in time, to a physical object, the sea. An hour isn't really a long time, but when she compares it to the wide, seemingly endless sea, it appears to be a lot longer. By showing readers how long an hour feels to the poem's speaker—to her, an hour is, truly, a sea—she suggests how the speaker feels: lonely, anxious, and impatient.

Accuracy   Take a look at these three lines:

> The wine-dark sea
> crashes onto the beach
> like bottles of broken Cabernet.

It's a pretty awful image: the writer has gone overboard in using figurative language. Just because *wine-dark* is a metaphor for the color of the sea doesn't mean the writer has to follow up by extending the metaphor to broken bottles of wine. Think about it logically: waves don't physically crash down onto beaches the way bottles break, and the sounds don't match up. Waves are soft and appear over and over again; bottles shatter with a single loud sound, in a one-time event. The word *crashes* doesn't seem exactly right. For figurative language to be effective, every word needs to be carefully chosen. Take a look at this revision:

> The wine-dark sea
> slides into the beach
> like spilled soda.

That's still not brilliant poetry, especially since the poet has mixed "wine" with "soda" in the same metaphor, but it works a bit better because the images make more sense: the sea fizzes and sputters, just like spilled soda, as it reaches the beach.

That's more accurate than crashing and broken bottles. Remember: figurative language doesn't have to be grand; it just has to be accurate.

Avoid Mixed Metaphors

A mixed metaphor is what you get when you join two unrelated metaphors. Mixed metaphors sometimes occur when you don't think carefully about the meaning of your words, such as in the following examples:

> He really hit that hot potato out of the park.
> His argument crescendoed as he hammered home his point.
> He poured forth his story with his heart in his mouth.

If you try to imagine what's going on in these sentences, you can't—the mixed metaphors create illogical, confusing, and sometimes contradictory images. Mixed metaphors suggest carelessness: if you haven't chosen your images deliberately, you risk creating something unclear or illogical. When you write, stick to one metaphor.

Breaking the Rule   As usual, once you know the rule, you can think about breaking it. Take a look at these lines from Shakespeare's *Hamlet*:

> To be, or not to be: that is the question:
> Whether 'tis nobler in the mind to suffer
> The slings and arrows of outrageous fortune,

Or to take arms against a sea of troubles,
And by opposing end them?

This passage features a mixed metaphor that, not surprisingly, raises questions: how do you *take arms* against a *sea* of troubles? Is Hamlet suggesting that taking up arms would mean sure death, since you can't fight the sea? Is he thinking about suicide or getting revenge? Would he be killed if he took revenge on the king? Shakespeare didn't mix his metaphors by accident; he did it with a purpose: to demonstrate that many things can be possible at once (both suicide and revenge). Shakespeare was a master poet, and he used this mixed metaphor deliberately, to illustrate a complex idea.

Ultimate Style

Avoid Clichés

A cliché is a phrase that's trite and tired. You should do your best to avoid clichés in your poems—they don't evoke any new ideas, images, or feelings. Clichés often take the form of comparisons, such as "strong as an ox." If a comparison is used often enough, it actually loses its meaning—you can no longer imagine what's going on. Here are some examples:

Blind as a bat
Pretty as a picture
Cute as a button

Clichés aren't always comparisons. Sometimes they're simply phrases that appear far too often, in far too many poems, such as the following:

> Blood-red flowers
> The moonlit water
> The river gently flows
> The ancient sea glitters

All of these sound tired and heavy-handed. If you're writing phrases like this, you're not writing poetry; you're stringing together clichés. One way to avoid clichés is to second-guess anything that comes to mind too easily. Think of a cat. How would you describe it? You might bring up furry, timid, haughty, coy, or soft. All those adjectives are obvious. What else is there to say about the cat? Was it born in the Himalayas and transported here by traders? That's a better subject for a poem about a cat; that trip would allow you to incorporate more vivid images, a story, and different kinds of adjectives about the mountains, the people, and the journey. It's not that you shouldn't write a poem about a cat—but what you should do is flip your idea upside down and look at it from other angles.

Employ Allusion

Allusion is an indirect reference to something else. If you've ever referred to a difficult, lose-lose situation as a "catch-22," you're alluding to Joseph Heller's novel, *Catch-22*. Or perhaps you've heard someone described as a "Falstaffian" character—

this is an allusion to Falstaff, a character from Shakespeare's work, and it means that the person is an unmanageable, unfettered, wild, and possibly criminal. Understanding allusions such as these means understanding the literary works from which they're drawn. If you don't know what Falstaff is like, for example, learning that someone is "Falstaffian" is meaningless. When you allude to something in a poem, you assume your readers will know what you're referring to. Allusion can add richness and depth to your work: by alluding to something, you automatically bring the associated images, stories, events, and feelings into your poem.

Ultimate Style

Take a look at how Keats uses allusion in these lines from "Ode to a Nightingale":

> My heart aches, and a drowsy numbness pains
> My sense, as though of hemlock I had drunk

Here, Keats expects the reader to know that Socrates was forced to commit suicide by drinking hemlock (a poison) and to associate it here with wisdom and noble sacrifice.

Alluding for a Reason In many cases, allusion makes readers work harder, since they have to understand not only your poem but also your references. Being referential is, in this way, being an intelligent, well-read writer. However, take care not to include a slew of allusions in your poems just for the sake of being "smart"—you'll no doubt hurt the poem and lose your readers. Use allusion when it's appropriate: when the thing you're referring to really moves you or when it makes sense for the meaning of the poem.

Use Hyperbole and Understatement

Hyperbole is an overstatement or exaggeration, such as "I ate tons of french fries." In poetry, hyperbole is useful when you want to emphasize the importance, significance, or drama of an idea, event, or thought without saying outright, "This is really important." Walt Whitman uses hyperbole in this line from "Song of Myself":

For every atom belonging to me as good belongs to you

We understand immediately how fully he believes in the community he's discussing—he believes that even atoms belong to both him and others. No one can literally share an atom, but his hyperbole emphasizes this sense of universality.

You can also use hyperbole to create humor in your poems, by exaggerating something absurdly, such as in this line from Shakespeare's *Macbeth*:

Here's the smell of the blood still: all the perfumes of Arabia will not sweeten this little hand.

Understatement is the opposite of hyperbole—as its name suggests, it is the minimization of an idea or thought. Understatement is useful when you want to offer select images, feelings, or ideas and let readers fill in the blanks. Most poems are evocative because of what's left out or left unsaid. William Blake uses understatement to make observations about time and death in "The Echoing Green":

Till the little ones, weary,
No more can be merry;
The sun does descend,
And our sports have an end.
Round the laps of their mothers
Many sisters and brothers,
Like birds in their nest,
Are ready for rest,
And sport no more seen
On the darkening Green.

Blake is not talking merely about "sports," or playing, on an "echoing green." He's making a larger statement about time—when the green darkens, as he says in the last line, he's referring to more than just the falling of night. Earlier in the poem, Blake talks about "old folk" who watch children playing on the green and feel nostalgic. Those children, in the stanza above, eventually become "weary" themselves, and the time of playing will one day end for them as well. By using understatement, Blake hints at the larger meaning to his poem without having to make explicit statements about the passing of time. You have to work a bit to understand what he's getting at.

Use Personification

When you give life to an inanimate object, you're using personification. You can use personification in a poem to present ideas or events from a fresh perspective or to make your images surprising. Take a look at how Percy Bysshe Shelley uses personification in "To Night":

Wrap thy form in a mantle grey,
  Star-inwrought!
Blind with thine hair the eyes of Day,
Kiss her until she be wearied out,
Then wander o'er city and sea and land,
Touching all with thine opiate wand–
  Come, long-sought!

Here, night takes on the characteristics of a bewitching force:
it wraps itself in "grey," kisses daytime, and wanders far and
wide, touching people with its "opiate wand." Instead of simply
describing night, Shelley addresses this poem to it and treats it
almost as a person, which is fresh and unexpected.

Learn Other Figures of Speech

Similes and metaphors are the types of figurative language
you'll use most often, but there are other techniques you can
use as well to give your poems some verve. As with all poetic
techniques, be careful not to overuse any one of these. Employ-
ing a variety of figures of speech, and using them deliberately
to make specific points, will result in a poem that is more
sophisticated than one that is overstuffed with supposed
cleverness.

Synecdoche/Metonymy   Synecdoche is using one part
of a thing to stand for the entire thing. For example, if you
say "The suits ate dinner at the pub," *suits* stands for men in
suits. T. S. Eliot's famous phrase, "I should have been a pair

of ragged claws // scuttling across the floors of silent seas," is synecdoche. *Claws* are just one part of the sea creature Eliot is conjuring here.

Metonymy is so similar to synecdoche that the two are often confused—but metonymy refers to a situation in which an attribute or suggestion of something stands for the actual thing. For example, if you point to a picture of a lion and a toddler responds, *RRRROOOAR*, he's referring to the lion by the sounds associated with it. A common example of metonymy employs the term "White House," as in:

Ultimate Style

The order issued from the White House.

The structure itself can't issue an order, and here, "White House" stands for the administrators—the actual people—who issue orders.

Synesthesia   Synesthesia, which means "blended or joined feeling" in Greek, occurs when two different senses are evoked together. In poetry, synesthesia generally occurs when a sensory attribute is given to something that does not actually have that sensory attribute. For example, look at these lines from Charles Baudelaire's "Correspondences":

The perfume is as fresh as the flesh of an infant
Sweet as an oboe, green as a prairie,
—And the others corrupt, rich and triumphant

We smell perfume, but we *hear* an oboe's sound—Baudelaire has blended two different senses. He also compares the same smell to the green of a prairie, but perfume, again, isn't visual—it can't be green.

Figurative Language in Action

In "The Fish," Elizabeth Bishop uses figurative language very effectively. Though this poem focuses on catching a fish, there is another layer of meaning that Bishop achieves by using metaphors and similes.

The Fish

I caught a tremendous fish
and held him beside the boat
half out of water, with my hook
fast in a corner of its mouth.
He didn't fight.
He hadn't fought at all.
He hung a grunting weight,
battered and venerable
and homely. Here and there
his brown skin hung in strips
like ancient wallpaper,
and its pattern of darker brown
was like wallpaper:
shapes like full-blown roses
stained and lost through age.
He was speckled with barnacles,

fine rosettes of lime,

and infested

with tiny white sea-lice,

and underneath two or three

rags of green weed hung down.

While his gills were breathing in

the terrible oxygen

—the frightening gills,

fresh and crisp with blood,

that can cut so badly—

I thought of the coarse white flesh

packed in like feathers,

the big bones and the little bones,

the dramatic reds and blacks

of his shiny entrails,

and the pink swim-bladder

like a big peony.

I looked into his eyes

which were far larger than mine

but shallower, and yellowed,

the irises backed and packed

with tarnished tinfoil

seen through the lenses

of old scratched isinglass.

They shifted a little, but not

to return my stare.

—It was more like the tipping

of an object toward the light.

I admired his sullen face,

the mechanism of his jaw,

and then I saw

that from his lower lip

—if you could call it a lip—

grim, wet, and weaponlike,

hung five old pieces of fish-line,

or four and a wire leader

with the swivel still attached,

with all their five big hooks

grown firmly in his mouth.

A green line, frayed at the end

where he broke it, two heavier lines,

and a fine black thread

still crimped from the strain and snap

when it broke and he got away.

Like medals with their ribbons

frayed and wavering,

a five-haired beard of wisdom

trailing from his aching jaw.

I stared and stared

and victory filled up

the little rented boat,

from the pool of bilge

where oil had spread a rainbow

around the rusted engine

to the bailer rusted orange,

the sun-cracked thwarts,

the oarlocks on their strings,

the gunnels—until everything

was rainbow, rainbow, rainbow!

And I let the fish go.

In this poem, the act of catching a fish works as a metaphor for a personal struggle the speaker is finally coming to terms with—a stubborn issue, as stubborn as the old fish with five hooks in his mouth. Bishop uses many similes: she compares the fish's skin and pattern to wallpaper, flesh to feathers, swimbladder to peony. The poem is filled with specifics. We can see that fish perfectly clearly.

Beyond the idea of struggle, the meaning of the poem remains ambiguous. It could be about victory ("victory filled up the little rented boat") and conquest—the traditional conquest of man over nature. Perhaps Bishop is saying that a woman, unlike a man, would not kill the great old fish but instead let it go—a feminist statement. Perhaps she's saying that despite the brutality of fishing, the brutality of age (the fish's age), and the oil leaking from the boat's engine, everything is "rainbow, rainbow, rainbow!"—in other words, something beautiful, essential, or important exists there despite the problems and unpleasantness. Perhaps the poem is about death and the acceptance of it, with the rainbows the final illumination, or, simply, heaven.

Good poems usually incorporate irony or ambiguity, so more than one meaning might be accurate. Often the true "meaning" of a poem may be in the question the poem raises. Bishop's poem may be about beating inner conflict, or it may be about coming to terms with death; both are possibilities. The success of the poem resides in the images Bishop creates, not in one single meaning.

Ultimate Style

Exercises

- Make a list of the first five cliché comparisons that come to your mind. Now create new, fresh similes or metaphors that convey the same idea for each one.

- Write a short poem in which you describe a broken heart by describing the end of a dinner party. Don't mention love, heartbreak, or sadness—but convey them by using thoughtful similes and metaphors.

- Write a short poem using personification. Give life to your favorite handbag, your bicycle, a tree in your backyard, or something you own that no one else knows you have.

Imagery

Every poem you write should include imagery, which is simply vivid word-pictures. Imagery links words to the senses and makes your readers both envision and feel what you're writing. Images can make an abstract idea concrete. It's less interesting to hear the word *apple* than to see it, touch it, smell it, and eat it. It's through the physical attributes of the apple that we understand and appreciate it. Likewise, creating physical, vivid images will help your readers understand and appreciate your poems.

Keep in mind that an image itself isn't a poem: an image is something we see or feel. When you use an image, you convey an idea more beautifully than you would by simply saying what you mean, and you help readers understand an idea more deeply. Poetry isn't about telling people things; it's about expressing yourself in a distinguished or unusual way.

Use Concrete Images

All images should be concrete—in other words, they should represent something you can see and touch. It's difficult for a reader to understand what you're talking about if you write only in the abstract. That's why poets use images to convey all sorts of things. We live in a physical world; we feel through our senses and understand the world through the objects in it.

Here's a famously brief and imagistic poem by Ezra Pound, called "In a Station of the Metro":

> The apparition of these faces in the crowd;
>> Petals on a wet, black bough.

Here, we can *see* the faces that Pound is talking about. However, Pound's poem is about more than faces and petals. The stark image of the petals on the bough suggests the loneliness that can be felt even in the middle of a crowd. Instead of telling us that the poem is about loneliness, Pound creates a concrete image to convey it more beautifully.

Ultimate Style

Use Appropriate Images

Make sure your images work in the context of what you're writing about. Even if an image is incredibly beautiful, it won't help your poem if it doesn't fit your subject matter. Images should be part of the very fabric of your poem, and if an image isn't appropriate, it'll stand out, distract your readers, and diminish your poem's effectiveness.

If you're writing a poem about a happy marriage, you'll probably include hopeful images, not dark ones. Similarly, if you're writing about death, it wouldn't be wise to include gorgeous images of lush flowers. Neither would it be appropriate to include images that relate to fabric and sewing. Make sure your images work in the context of what you're writing about. A marriage poem would benefit greatly from lots of images

about fabric and sewing—you could stitch together a poem, or
an item of clothing, the way you'd imagine stitching together a
marriage.

Philip Levine uses a vast array of appropriate images in
this excerpt from "Salts and Oils":

> A mile from Ebbets Field, from all
> that history, I found Murray, my papa's
> buddy, in his greasy truck shop, polishing
> replacement parts. Short, unshaven, puffed,
> he strutted the filthy aisles,
> a tiny Ghengis Khan. He sent out for soup
> and sandwiches. The world turned on barley,
> pickled meats, yellow mustard, kasha,
> rye breads.

Levine is known for writing poems about his immigrant,
Jewish, working-class, background. One image after another
reflects the time and situation of the poem, and him in it.
He refers to masculine, domestic details such as trucks and
replacement parts. He's not writing in a high, elevated style.
Levine also evokes his Jewish past with images of barley,
pickled meats, yellow mustard, kasha, and rye breads. All the
images he uses in this poem are appropriate not only to the
subject matter, but to him. He has so particular a style that if
you look at a Levine poem, the rough, working-class immigrant
images make it obvious who the author is, and in this case why
that year has such resonance for him.

Don't Go Overboard

Take a look at these three image-laden lines:

> Clouds in the blue-gray sky, reversed in the lake,
> shift then flip and disperse, in cotton-puff trails and swirls
> or it thickens into long, gold-edged soap bubbles.

Image overload! One image would have been enough, but here they're piled on top of each other. Instead of seeing one cloud doing one specific thing, you see many different clouds changing forms, and you imagine each of them. Then the cotton puff appears, and then the clouds become soap bubbles. This multitude of images isn't impressive: it reveals a beginner poet. A good poem shows restraint and exactitude. One perfect image is much more effective than many careless ones thrown together.

Ultimate Style

Use Symbols

A symbol is an image that stands for something else. With metaphors, the image itself is important—but with symbols, we're interested in the thing the symbol stands for, not in the symbol itself. For example, a red rose is a traditional symbol of love or romance. Whenever a red rose in mentioned, you should be more interested in what the rose stands for than you are in the rose itself. Using symbols in your poem can create deeper layers of meaning, beyond the words on the page.

Symbols can sometimes work against you if you fail to be original. For example, a red rose as a symbol for love is so overused that it's become a cliché—this type of overt symbolism won't really add anything valuable to your poems. Symbols don't have to be so direct—sometimes making your readers do a little guesswork can make your poem more effective. You can incorporate symbols the same way you incorporate images or metaphors, in a subtle way that requires your readers to consider your words carefully.

Take a look at these two stanzas from Keats's famous "Ode to a Nightingale," which centers on one of the most famous and complex symbols in literature:

Stanza 1:

My heart aches, and a drowsy numbness pains
 My sense, as though of hemlock I had drunk,
Or emptied some dull opiate to the drains
 One minute past, and Lethe-wards had sunk:
'Tis not through envy of thy happy lot,
 But being too happy in thine happiness,
 That thou, light-wingèd Dryad of the trees,
  In some melodious plot
Of beechen green, and shadows numberless,
 Singest of summer in full-throated ease.

Stanza 6:

Darkling I listen; and, for many a time
 I have been half in love with easeful Death,
Call'd him soft names in many a musèd rhyme,

To take into the air my quiet breath;

Now more than ever seems it rich to die,

To cease upon the midnight with no pain,

While thou art pouring forth thy soul abroad

In such an ecstasy!

Still wouldst thou sing, and I have ears in vain—

To thy high requiem become a sod.

The nightingale is a conflicted symbol of death and release. As he listens, his heart aches and a "drowsy numbness" pains his sense. In the second stanza, Keats says: "That I might drink, and leave the world unseen, and with thee fade away into the forest dim." Is he suicidal? In the next few stanzas, he uses other images: embalmèd darkness, fast-fading violets, murmurous haunt of flies. Then he states his death wish outright in stanza six: "I have been half in love with easeful Death ..."

In stanza six, things change. He calls the nightingale's song a "requiem" and realizes that to the bird's requiem he will become a sod. That version of death is very different from the pain-free, joyful version of the previous stanzas. Before the nightingale was a symbol of death; now it's singing a requiem for his death. Suddenly, the seriousness of mortality becomes clear. This change complicates the symbol: is the bird a symbol of death or of life? A bird singing a requiem is a symbol of nature, of earthly life that continues once we're gone. The brilliance of Keats's poem is his ability to create a symbol and then turn it around to suggest something different and more complicated.

Imagery in Action

Sylvia Plath's "Morning Song" is about the birth of a child, a heady, profoundly physical event, and she uses concrete images to enliven the poem and reveal the event more clearly, as well as to represent abstract concepts.

Morning Song

Love set you going like a fat gold watch.
The midwife slapped your footsoles, and your bald cry
Took its place among the elements.

Our voices echo, magnifying your arrival. New statue.
In a drafty museum, your nakedness
Shadows our safety. We stand round blankly as walls.

I'm no more your mother
Than the cloud that distills a mirror to reflect its own slow
Effacement at the wind's hand.

All night your moth-breath
Flickers among the flat pink roses. I wake to listen:
A far sea moves in my ear.

One cry, and I stumble from bed, cow-heavy and floral
In my Victorian nightgown.
Your mouth opens clean as a cat's. The window square

> Whitens and swallows its dull stars. And now you try
> Your handful of notes;
> The clear vowels rise like balloons.

Throughout this poem, Plath uses concrete images, such as "your bald cry took its place among the elements." By preceding *cry* with *bald*, the elusive cry—which disappears, and which has no physicality—becomes real, attached to an infant. Plath has a habit of switching back and forth between lively images that reflect actual things and lively images that represent abstractions.

Ultimate Style

In the third stanza, Plath compares her motherhood to a cloud that's slowly disappearing. She doesn't just tell us how she feels: she uses the image of a cloud and a mirror to create an image that *reveals* how she feels. The fourth stanza discusses something very real: her child's breath, evoked as a "moth-breath" that "flickers among the fat pink roses." The lush, tangible images are far more effective than talking about a baby's breath. Then, one line later, she switches in a concrete image for an abstract idea again: "A far sea moves in my ear." Does she hear death? In the poem's brilliantly worded ending, "The clear vowels rise like balloons," we get both the abstract and the concrete. Vowels, which are uttered and then lost, literally rise like balloons.

Exercises

• Categorize the images in "Morning Song" into each of the five senses.

• Think of specific, concrete images (a phrase or a sentence) to describe each of the following without stating them directly: anger, leisure time, wealth, and poverty.

• Write a few lines that that use the image of fire in a distinctive way. Describe the setting, the kind of fire, the color of the flame, the heat generated by the fire, and the people (or lack of people) nearby.

Lines and Line Breaks

Poems are made up of lines—sometimes as few as two lines or even one, sometimes as many as several hundred. The basic structural element of a poem is the line, comparable to the sentence in prose. Put enough sentences together and you get a story or a novel; put enough lines together and you have a poem. Every single line matters in a poem. Each is its own little work of art.

Keep in mind that a line isn't necessarily a sentence—in most cases, it won't be. It may be part of a sentence, a phrase, a group of carefully linked words, or even a single word. There are no limits to what shape your line can take. But there *are* some guidelines you can keep in mind to make each and every line in your poem as striking as possible.

6

Control Line Length

When you're reading poetry out loud, you'll notice that lines in many poems are more or less equal to a breath. Keeping your lines to a reasonable length makes them easier to read out loud and helps you put your ideas across in an unintimidating, accessible way. However, you'll see just as many poems with very long lines and very short lines. There's a time and a place for all kinds of line lengths, and figuring out how long the lines in your own poems should be is a learning process. Try your poem one way, then change the structure and try the poem another way, with longer or shorter lines. Pretty soon you'll get it.

Using Long Lines   If you have a lot of material to include in your poem and if you want to give your poem a grand, sweeping effect, you might choose to use long lines. The poet Walt Whitman is famous for his very long lines, such as in these lines from a poem called "Mannahatta":

> Immigrants arriving, fifteen or twenty thousand in a week,
> The carts hauling goods—the manly race of drivers of horses—
>   the brown-faced sailors,
> The summer air, the bright sun shining, and the sailing
>   clouds aloft,
> The winter snows, the sleigh-bells—the broken ice in the
>   river, passing along up or down with the flood-tide or
>   ebb-tide,
> The mechanics of the city, the masters, well-form'd,
>   beautiful-faced, looking you straight in the eyes,

Whitman's long, unfettered lines are full of lists that include everything: city life, immigrants, scenes of snow, vehicles, architecture, boats. Those long lines work because of what's inside them. He needed space to convey the things and images he wanted to. Short lines would have been much less effective:

> Immigrants arriving,
> fifteen or twenty thousand
> in a week,

> The carts hauling goods—
> the manly race of drivers of horses—
> the brown-faced sailors

You'd get tired of reading quickly because the lines aren't long or dense enough.

Using Shorter Lines Using shorter lines draws more close attention to individual things, ideas, words, and phrases. Visually, everything in the line stands out more clearly—there's less clutter. When you read the poem out loud, there's more breathing room. Take a look at these lines from Ralph Waldo Emerson's "Song of Nature":

> Mine are the night and morning,
> The pits of air, the gulf of space,
> The sportive sun, the gibbous moon,
> The innumerable days.

Emerson is far more restrained than Whitman, and his lines are short. Emerson is conveying a list as well, but his list has fewer adjectives, and each line is balanced. "The pits of air" and "the gulf of space" both have monosyllables and the same rhythm. "The sportive sun" and "the gibbous moon" are also balanced: *sportive*, like *gibbous*, is two syllables, and *sun*, like *moon*, is one syllable. Emerson's poem would not work as well in longer lines:

> Mine are the night and morning, the pits of air, the gulf of space,
> The sportive sun, the gibbous moon, the innumerable days.

There are too many monosyllables, and the poem sounds like a nursery rhyme. When everything is on one line, you read it faster, and you lose the significance and weight of the individual words.

Break Lines Carefully

A line break is exactly what it sounds like: it's where you break, or end, a line of poetry. You may think that poetry is simply prose broken up into lines, but that's far from the truth. Creating a line with a natural beginning and end is a skill you must learn and practice. Take a look at what happens when we simply break prose up into lines:

Ultimate Style

> A line break
> is exactly what it sounds like:
> it's where you end
> a line of poetry.

This definitely isn't a poem: there's no excitement, no skill, and no rhythm. There's more to writing a poem than hitting the ENTER key every once in a while.

So where *should* you break a line? A good rule of thumb is to read the line out loud and end it when your breath ends naturally. But there are other things to consider as well. You may choose to break a line to give a certain effect, or you may break a line to follow a certain form or rhythm. There are no hard-and-fast rules about what makes a "perfect" line break. Do what feels right to you rhythmically—don't force a line to continue or to end. While it's important to have energetic, exciting line breaks and interestingly paced lines, that doesn't mean you should make every line break a violent one. Skill lies in varying your line breaks.

Enjambed Lines   Enjambment occurs when there is no punctuation at the end of a line. Enjambment has nothing to do with whether or not an actual *sentence* ends—rather, enjambment concerns only punctuation. If there is no punctuation at the end of a line, the line is considered enjambed. Take a look at the use of enjambment in this verse by William Blake:

> Abstinence sows sand all over
> The ruddy limbs & flaming hair,
> But Desire Gratified
> Plants fruits of life & beauty there.

Lines one and three are enjambed—there is no punctuation at the ends of them. Lines two and four are not enjambed, since they end with a comma and a period, respectively. In this poem, you still pause at the end of each line. The line breaks set the pace of the poem, and the lines are balanced—you neither speed up nor slow down as you read.

Other times enjambment is more forceful and pushes one line quickly and energetically to the next line, speeding up the end of the sentence. See how Gerard Manley Hopkins handles this in his poem 47:

My own heart let me have more pity on; let

Me live to my sad self hereafter kind,

Charitable; not live this tormented mind

With this tormented mind tormenting yet.

 I cast for comfort I can no more get

By groping round my comfortless, than blind

Eyes in their dark can day or thirst can find

Thirst's all-in-all in all a world of wet.

Soul, self; come, poor Jackself, I do advise

You, jaded, let be; call off thoughts awhile

Elsewhere; leave comfort root-room; let joy size

At God knows when to God knows what; whose smile

's not wrung, see you; unforeseen times rather—as skies

Betweenpie mountains—lights a lovely mile.

Ultimate Style

In the first line, Hopkins pauses with a semicolon *before* the end of the line, but once he's at the end of the line he rushes forward to the next one. Some lines are enjambed, others are not, which is a good way to vary a poem. Then, expertly, Hopkins enjambs violently in line six, with "blind eyes." If you're reading out loud, you'll see that you can't really pause after "blind." You must move quickly to the beginning of the next line, to "eyes"—and the emphasis is on "eyes."

Aggressive enjambment occurs in other places as well. In the first two lines of the second stanza, where he says "I do advise // You, jaded," he forces the line over on "advise" to "you," and then he adds one comma after another to slow the line down. That contributes to the rhythm. Hopkins also gets bold with "smile" in line twelve. First you think there's a pause, and then, when you get to the beginning of the next line, you're forced to elide (omit) the beginning of the line, with the apostrophe-s, and move quickly into the next line. Hopkins is expert at using enjambment to spice up his poems and to control the pacing.

End-Stopped Lines Any line that has punctuation at the end of it—a comma, period, exclamation, semicolon, dash—is called an end-stopped line. It forces you either to pause or to curtail the flow of a poem. Take a look at how twentieth-century poet Constantine Cavafy uses end-stopped lines to great effect in "In the Same Space":

> The surroundings of home, centers, neighborhoods
> which I see and where I walk; for years and years.
>
> I have created you in joy and in sorrows:
> Out of so many circumstances, out of so many things.
>
> You have become all feeling for me.

This poem is made up of a list, and it's very emotional. More important, it's made up almost entirely of end-stopped lines. You get a stop-and-start feeling from reading them: the sentences are short, and they pile up. The result is suspenseful. It's not clear whether the things he's listing are hopeful or sad. Did he share them with someone? Or did he wish he shared them and live instead with his desire? The final wrap-it-up line, when we discover that the "you" is "entirely a feeling, for me," brings those moments together. We (and the speaker) come away with something, even if it's just a feeling. If every line were enjambed and the structure were more flowing, we wouldn't get that sense of suspense.

Control Pace

The pace, or speed, of your poem depends heavily on line breaks. The end of a line often signals a pause, which can slow the pace down. Longer lines that run together can speed up the pace. The pace of your poem should match your subject matter. A quick, flitting pace for a poem about the end of a love affair wouldn't make as much sense at a slower, more pensive pace. Take a look at a poem called "Water" by Philip Larkin, without the line breaks:

Ultimate Style

> If I were called in to construct a religion I should make use of water. Going to church would entail a fording to dry, different clothes; my litany would employ images of sousing, a furious devout drench, and I should raise in the east a glass of water where any-angled light would congregate endlessly.

Now read the actual poem, with the line breaks:

> If I were called in
> To construct a religion
> I should make use of water.

Going to church
Would entail a fording
To dry, different clothes;

My litany would employ
Images of sousing,
A furious devout drench,

And I should raise in the east
A glass of water
Where any-angled light
Would congregate endlessly.

All the line breaks make the poem weightier, and they slow down the pace of the poem. If you read it as a paragraph, it goes a lot more quickly. The emphasis on certain words gets lost, and there are no pauses to make you stop and think. In the actual poem, you see and feel the images much more strongly—the line breaks draw you into the poem.

How do you decide how to pace your poem, and whether to enjamb or end-stop a line? Much of your decision will be intuitive. But one good method is to keep reading your poem out loud. Write a few lines, then read them out loud. If your poem sounds plodding or dull, you probably need to fiddle with the lines. Try varying the number of end-stopped lines. Break a phrase over the edge of a line and see if it makes a difference. Similarly, to add more balance to an overwhelming poem, even out the lines and make sure some are end-stopped, which will ensure that the pace is varied. Keep experimenting.

Give Lines Integrity

When a line has integrity, it makes sense independently, even if it consists of parts of two different sentences: the end of one sentence and the beginning of another. Line integrity is a way of keeping your lines smart and relevant. Look how Percy Bysshe Shelley uses line integrity in this excerpt from his poem "Ode to the West Wind":

The tumult of thy mighty harmonies

Ultimate Style

Will take from both a deep, autumnal tone,
Sweet though in sadness. Be thou, Spirit fierce,
My spirit! Be thou me, impetuous one!

The line "Sweet though in sadness. Be thou, Spirit fierce," includes parts of two sentences—one from the previous line, and one that starts on this line and continues to the next line. However, this line also reads like its own sentence, as though Shelley is imploring this spirit to be sweet as well as sad. The line has a meaning all its own.

Not every line can stand alone, nor should it. But you should pay attention to where your sentences begin and end and take care to add value to your poems through line integrity when you see an opportunity. Line integrity makes your poem stronger and more deliberate—a sign of expertise. It shows you've thought about the line itself, not just about what you're saying or what your sentences sound like. The "line" and the "sentence" are two different beasts, and you should consider both when you're writing a poem.

Pause Carefully

Pauses in lines of poetry are called **caesuras**. At best, caesuras knock you off balance and add music to a line. You can use them to make your poetry thoughtful, powerful, rhythmic, and suspenseful. At worst, caesuras make your line move like a see-saw:

> The phone book sits, the numbers list
> The people's names, and their addresses.

A comma usually indicates a caesura, but a caesura may also be a pause with no grammatical markings, or a period where the sentence ends. Caesuras can appear at the beginning, in the middle, or at the end of a line (initial, medial, and terminal caesuras, respectively). You can use any number of caesuras in a line, or none at all.

This passage from John Donne's "Holy Sonnet VII," written in 1633, uses initial, medial, and terminal caesuras:

> At the round earth's imagined corners, blow
> Your trumpets, angels, and arise, arise
> From death, you numberless infinities
> Of souls, and to your scattered bodies go,

The terminal caesura, noted by the comma between *corners* and *blow* on the first line, is more than just a pause. It's right before the command, *blow,* so you pause, catch your breath, and then physically *blow.*

The medial caesura after *angels,* in line 2, is a pause between a command to the angels to follow two actions: blow and arise.

The initial caesuras, in the third and fourth lines, indicated by commas after *death* and *souls,* force you to pause at two important parts. You pause after *death,* which is fitting: death itself *is* a pause. The pause after *souls* is also important because that's how you realize what the angels are—they're the numberless infinities, the souls. The emphasis on the word *souls* indicates what the poem is all about.

Ultimate Style

Contradictions   Caesuras can be useful for presenting contradicting ideas. In the poem "Epistle II," Alexander Pope uses medial caesuras to separate opposing ideas:

> Created half to rise, and half to fall;
> Great lord of all things, yet a prey to all

Each half of the line, separated by a comma, contradicts the other half. The subject of the poem is both rising and falling, both lord and prey. Pope sets up these oppositions clearly by separating them with pauses.

Important Ideas   Caesuras can often simply call attention to something important. William Wordsworth uses a caesura effectively in the final stanza of "She Dwelt among the Untrodden Ways":

> She lived unknown, and few could know
> > When Lucy ceased to be;
> But she is in her grave, and, oh,
> > The difference to me!

Wordsworth breaks up the regular meter of his lines to insert the *oh*, and the commas around it ensure that the reader pauses before moving on to the next line. This slight break in the rhythm calls attention to the final thought: that Lucy's death means a great deal to the speaker, even though she was unknown to many other people. The caesura emphasizes this point.

Lines and Line Breaks in Action

William Carlos Williams's poem "The Red Wheelbarrow" is a masterful example of skillful lines and line breaks.

The Red Wheelbarrow

so much depends
upon

a red wheel
barrow

glazed with rain
water

beside the white
chickens.

The entire poem is one sentence, and you can see that "so much depends" on each word and each line break. Because the sentence is so slow-moving, spread across eight lines, each word has weight.

The poem is painterly—instead of thinking about a concept, you imagine the wheelbarrow. You see how it gets glazed with rainwater, and you see white chickens beside it. It's kind of like a still-life painting. And Williams is careful with his line breaks—he breaks each line at the best, most inevitable place. *Upon* gets its own line—it physically rests upon the blank space, giving that space more pause and significance. Then he breaks after *wheel*—why not after *wheelbarrow*? By leaving the word unfinished, he forces a surprise: you know very little about the wheel until the next line, when you realize it's actually a wheelbarrow.

Williams uses the same technique in the following lines: "glazed with rain // water." Why not just say "glazed with rainwater"? That's too easy. True, rain and rainwater are the same, but Williams forces you to hang on *water*, giving it more emphasis.

Ultimate Style

Exercises

- Write four end-stopped lines of poetry. Then rewrite the same four lines in a way that uses enjambment. Finally, vary the lines between end-stopped and enjambed lines.

- Create two instances of violent enjambment, of two lines each. Try to use verbs at the ends or beginnings of the line.

- Write a Whitmanesque poem that consists of a list, with very long lines, scattered thoughts here and there, excitement, and some higher meaning to it all. The list can include anything— you can be shopping for shoes or fruit, thinking about war-torn countries, or describing a walk through a forest.

Rhyme

Don't fall prey to naïve rhymes. Expertly done, rhymes can transform a poem from something that's just okay into a witty, fun, or ironic piece of writing. Nursery rhymes got their name for a reason: they're so simple that they amuse children, and they read like songs. In fact, rhyme was originally used to help people remember poems, or songs, before there was paper to record them. When you memorize a poem with rhymes, it's easier to get from one line to the next.

Rhyming has a place in sophisticated poetry as well, and it can contribute a great deal to a poem's effectiveness and impact. Rhymes help emphasize ideas, connect words to each other, and enhance the musical sound of a poem. Even though you might associate rhyming with simple poems, rhymes can actually be complex and nuanced. Rhyming well is a skill you can learn.

7

Learn the Types

There are three main types of rhymes:

1. Pure rhymes
2. Slant rhymes
3. Internal rhymes

Each type of rhyme creates a different effect in your poem,
and you can use each type deliberately to create the sound and
effect you want.

Pure Rhymes   Pure rhymes have the same number of
syllables and sound exactly alike except for one letter: *day/say*,
meet/greet, *sappy/happy*. These types of rhymes are the ones
used in nursery rhymes and many songs, but they can also be
used to create sophisticated, effective poems. Just be careful
not to overuse them.

Robert Frost uses pure rhymes in these lines from his
poem "October":

> O hushed October morning mild,
> Thy leaves have ripened to the fall;
> Tomorrow's wind, if it be wild,
> Should waste them all.

Mild/wild and *fall/all* are pure rhymes, but Frost manages to
keep his poem from sounding like a nursery rhyme. He does
this by varying line length to give the poem some texture. The
fourth line is significantly shorter than the others, and it has
only two accents (on the words *waste* and *all*) instead of the
four accents common to the other sentences. This difference
gives the line punch and emphasis and makes it sound abrupt,
not singsongy.

You don't always have to make every other line rhyme.
Sometimes the rhymes occur more sporadically. Take a look at
these lines from Robert Lowell's "1958":

> Remember standing with me in the dark,
> escaping? In the wild house? Everything–
> I mad, you mad for me? And brought my ring
> that twelvecarat lunk of gold there . . . Joan of Arc,
> undeviating still to the true mark?

Lowell's rhymes are pure: *dark/Arc/mark, Everything/ring*. But they occur unexpectedly, without the smooth, even rhythm that we saw in the Frost poem. Lowell is rough and tense, with lots of stop-and-start phrases. His rhymes jump out at us and make the poem energetic.

Slant Rhymes   A slant rhyme occurs when the sounds of words match up closely, but they don't match exactly. These aren't the kinds of rhymes you see in nursery rhymes: instead of the pure rhyme *sun/fun*, for example, you might use the slanted rhyme *sun/insane*. The *s* and *n* sounds connect to each other and create a slant rhyme.

John Donne uses slant rhymes in the first few lines of "The Broken Heart":

> He is starke mad, who ever sayes,
>   That he hath been in love an houre,
> Yet not that love so soone decayes,
>   But that it can tenne in lesse space devour;
> But who will believe mee, if I sweare
> That I have had the plague a yeare?

Sayes is similar to *decayes*—they both end in *ayes*—but the sounds aren't exactly alike, so they form a slant rhyme. *Houre* and *devour* form a pure rhyme, but this is quickly followed with *sweare* and *yeare*, which are slant rhymes. These slant rhymes allow the lines of the poem to be connected musically, without seeming forced.

Here are some expert examples of slant rhymes:

nooses	exclusive
again	gain
cash	mustache
language	ridge
factories	breeze
direction	duration
kick	rhetoric
fine	feign

Internal Rhymes   You can make your poem musical by rhyming internally, within lines, rather than at the end of lines. Internal rhymes can be either slant or pure. You can use end-rhymes and internal rhymes together, or internal rhymes only. Either way, it makes the poem more fun to read.

Percy Bysshe Shelley uses internal rhymes in "The Cloud":

I bring fresh showers for the thirsting flowers

Shelley uses pure rhymes in this line, with *showers* and *flowers*. In this particular poem, Shelley goes on to use end-rhymes as well, but internal rhymes add another musical layer to the poem.

Rhyme in Forms

When you read rhymes in a poem that's written in a form, such as a sonnet, the rhymes occur very regularly. This pattern is called a **rhyme scheme**, and you can write it out with letters, such as ABAB CDCD EFEF GG. That means the first line rhymes with the third, the second with the fourth, and so on. When figuring out the rhyme scheme of a poem, you just match up the letters to track the rhymes. Each new letter means a new rhyme. Some forms, such as sonnets, require you to follow a particular, exact rhyme scheme. Even in strict forms, however, the rhymes can be pure or slant. Even though you have to assign letters to the words that rhyme, there's still room for flexibility.

Check out the rhyme scheme in the Shakespeare's well-known Sonnet 18:

Shall I compare thee to a summer's day?
Thou art more lovely and more temperate:
Rough winds do shake the darling buds of May,
And summer's lease hath all too short a date:
Sometime too hot the eye of heaven shines,
And often is his gold complexion dimmed;
And every fair from fair sometime declines,

> By chance or nature's changing course untrimmed;
> But thy eternal summer shall not fade
> Nor lose possession of that fair thou ow'st;
> Nor shall death brag thou wander'st in his shade
> When in eternal lines to time thou grow'st;
> So long as men can breathe or eyes can see,
> So long lives this, and this gives life to thee.

The rhyme scheme here is ABAB, CDCD, EFEF, GG. Many are pure rhymes, like *day/May* and *dimmed/untrimmed*. But there is also a slant rhyme, *temperate/date*. Shakespeare is also not forcing each line to end with a rhyming word; he's letting the lines push over onto the next lines without making the rhymes sound forced. That's the difference between rhyming thoughtlessly and rhyming thought*fully*. His rhymes enhance and control what's being said—he isn't rhyming as an afterthought just to fit the requirements of the form.

Ultimate Style

Rhyme Meaningfully

You can use rhymes to make a point, to contradict yourself, or to create emphasis. You can also use them to convey ideas that are witty, emotional, or otherwise interesting. If you see the rhyme *marry/wary*, read between the lines: there's a message in the rhyme. If you see the rhyme *me/eternity*, it suggests reflection, probably about death or growing older. If you see the rhyme *room/honeymoon*, you sense something risqué. Similarly, *love/enough* suggests a question: *is* love enough? The rhymes in the first stanza of the poem "Constancy" by George

Herbert create their own story with the poem and underscore the poem's theme of what defines a truly upright, honest man:

> Who is the honest man?
> He that doth still and strongly good pursue,
> To God, his neighbour, and himself most true:
> Whom neither force nor fawning can
> Unpin, or wrench from giving all their due.

The rhymes *man/can* and *pursue/true/due* tell the story. *Man can* be righteous and honest, if you *pursue* what's *true* you get your *due*.

Herbert isn't just writing a poem about it takes to be an honest man; he's charting the course of the honest man through the rhymes. It takes a skilled and thoughtful hand to intertwine the rhymes so precisely into the theme, but Herbert did this with his famously simple, straightforward language, without making the rhymes or thoughts seem strained. The poem has integrity as a whole—from the ideas down to the nitty-gritty rhymes—not just in its parts.

Rhyme in Action

In Diane Mehta's "Black Paper," the rhymes have a particular purpose: to give something sad and shaky a structure. This is a poem about someone's death—the "black paper."

Black Paper

Limbo comes with daylight at six;
she exits my longing, shifts

like the sea at dawn into simpler
things I'd like to believe will find me later.

She will find me later
among the greater

intentions, in moments of believing
she is closer when I'm grieving.

I listen in silence to her sounds,
it shakes my soul to the ground.

The hours are fixed, eclipsed
by her circumference.

The Jewish element looks for the Gestapo
in the shade, the rogue

wrong-impressions I cannot
evade fast enough, times I ought

not to have thought so much
about love; it was enough.

It is certain she will find me later,
I will meet her in the black paper

among the undulations
of ancient conversations,

Lots of poets use rhyme—or form or meter—as a buttress for
difficult material. The rhymes hold the poem together, but
they also hold the mourner together and become a way of
moving forward. The rhymes also suggest that death is rounded
or complete in some way. It's not open-ended chaos and
emptiness; rather, it's a place, with or without God, that has
a beginning (rhyme) and an end (rhyme) and that holds this
person inside.

Look at the refrain, "she will find me later." When the
speaker dies, she *will* meet the woman in the black paper,
among the "undulations of ancient conversations," or those of
their past and the historical past. Notice, too, how the pairing
of some rhymes is suggestive and gives you hints as to the
poem's meaning: later is greater, believing is grieving, sounds
are in the ground, the Gestapo (like death, as it meant death
for so many) is rogue, I cannot but I ought (not to have worried
about love), much is enough, and undulations are (in death)
conversations. The poet uses rhymes to imply further meanings
to what she actually puts on the page.

Exercises

- Think of five pure rhymes for the word *sea*, then use them to write a five-line poem with either end-rhymes or internal rhymes. Now think of five slant rhymes for the word "straight," then use them to write a five-line poem with either end-rhymes or internal rhymes.

- Write a poem using any number of internal rhymes (both slant and pure) but no end-rhymes.

Ultimate Style
- Write a poem using both internal and end-rhymes. Make sure your rhymes aren't forced—use them to add music and meaning to the poem.

Form

Form is the shape and structure of the poem. Form can be formal, such as a sonnet, or informal, such as free verse. You might think that poems written in a "form" are outdated—after all, many "classic" poets, such as Shakespeare, wrote in form, and many new, contemporary poems are written in free verse. However, understanding form—and trying it out with your own poems—is a good way to improve your writing.

A good modern dancer has probably first been trained in classical dance. And a good chef who creates weird, outlandish dishes is probably well trained in classic cooking methods. Similarly, a good poet is a trained poet. However you choose to write, you should know the basics first. A good education in form will certainly improve the structure of your poems and make them more successful, even if you ultimately choose to write in free verse. You need to know the rules before you can break or ignore them.

Understand the Stanza

A stanza is a unit in a poem, much like a paragraph. It's separated from the stanzas above and below it by a line of white space. There are three basic types of stanza in poetry, each of a different length:

1. *Quatrain*: four lines
2. *Tercet*: three lines
3. *Couplet*: two lines

There is no limit to how long a stanza can be, and you might choose to write a six-line stanza (*sestet*), an eight-line stanza (*octave*), or any other type. But quatrains, tercets, and couplets are the types you'll see most often. Besides length, the main difference among these types of stanza is in their tone and feeling. When choosing a stanza, consider what type of tone you want to convey. And remember that you can mix and match. A sonnet, for example, is composed of three quatrains and a couplet.

Quatrains   A quatrain seems powerful, weighty, and balanced, and it's a good choice for a very serious poem. Take a look at this stanza from "London" by William Blake:

> I wander thro' each charter'd street,
> Near where the charter'd Thames does flow,
> And mark in every face I meet
> Marks of weakness, marks of woe.

The quatrain helps create the perfect, rhythmic tone for a pensive poem about the unhappiness the speaker sees around him as he walks through London. This stanza type best suits the seriousness of the observations Blake makes. Beautiful, reflective poems fit well into quatrains. The quatrain is also a good format for treating something with ceremony, such as a death.

Tercets   The tercet, with its three-line structure, suggests motion, and it's conducive to a feeling of moving forward and pulling back. It's a good narrative form because it's not as heavy or dense as the quatrain, but it has more substance than the two-line couplet. Because it has three lines, the lines flow easily, one punching into the next line or stanza. You can keep winding in new thoughts.

Here's an example, from "The Triumph of Life" by Percy Bysshe Shelley:

> Swift as a spirit hastening to his task
> Of glory and of good, the Sun sprang forth
> Rejoicing in his splendour, and the mask

These are dynamic, forward-moving lines, full of meandering statements that snake around themselves and push forward.

Couplets   Couplets are excellent for irony and comedy, as well as for seeming lightheartedness about something that's really more emotional. Couplets are loose and light and can be adapted to many kinds of poems.

Alexander Pope's "Essay on Man" is written in couplets:

> Not one looks backward, onward still he goes,
> Yet ne'er looks forward farther than his nose.

Learn the Types

There are many types of standard poetic forms, such as
haiku, sonnets, and villanelles, but form isn't limited to preset
structures. Forms are flexible. If you write your entire poem
in four-line stanzas, or quatrains, those are a form. If you write
your poem in three-line stanzas, or tercets, those are a form.
The following list represents a selection of basic poetic forms,
but you may very well be writing in form without fitting into
one of these categories.

Villanelle   A villanelle is a tricky nineteen-line poem that always consists of five three-line stanzas followed by one four-line
stanza. There are two rhymes used throughout, and the rhyme
scheme is A1BA2 ABA1 ABA2 ABA1 ABA2 ABA1A2. Don't
let the rhyme scheme confuse you: essentially, there are two
different rhymed sounds that occur in a pattern throughout the
poem: A and B. Since two of the lines with the A rhyme (those
ending in *Villanelle* and *well*) are repeated throughout the
poem, we call these lines A1 and A2—this way, we know which
specific line appears where, and we know that these rhyming
A words are always the same. The other repeated rhyme is B.
Since the rhyming B words are always different, we don't need
to differentiate them with any numbers.

Take a look at this villanelle by W. E. Henley, called "A
Dainty Thing's the Villanelle," in which the poet discusses the
merits of the form:

A dainty thing's the Villanelle.
Sly, musical, a jewel in rhyme,
It serves its purpose passing well.

A double-clappered silver bell
That must be made to clink in chime,
A dainty thing's the Villanelle;

And if you wish to flute a spell,
Or ask a meeting 'neath the lime,
It serves its purpose passing well.

You must not ask of it the swell
Of organs grandiose and sublime –
A dainty thing's the Villanelle;

And, filled with sweetness, as a shell
Is filled with sound, and launched in time,
It serves its purpose passing well

Still fair to see and good to smell
As in the quaintness of its prime,
A dainty thing's the Villanelle,
It serves its purpose passing well.

Haiku   A haiku is a three-line, unrhymed Japanese form with lines consisting of five, seven, and five syllables. It isn't used very often in serious American poetry, but it's fun to experiment with. Here's an example:

Near spring in New York—
Flowers brighten wet cement,
Push through frozen ground.

Sestina   The sestina has six six-line stanzas followed by a three-line stanza. The first stanza is the defining one, because the words that end that stanza must be repeated as line endings in other stanzas, in different orders for each stanza. It's an exceptionally difficult form to master. For each succeeding stanza, the first line must end with the same word that ends the last line in the preceding stanza. The second line would repeat the word that ended the first line of the preceding stanza. The third line would repeat the word that ended the second-to-last line of the preceding stanza. The fourth line would repeat the word that ended the second line of the preceding stanza, and so on. The final three-line stanza must repeat the end words from the preceding (sixth) stanza's last three lines—which happens to be the end words from the first stanza's fifth, third, and first lines (in that order). But that last stanza must *also* include, in the interior of the stanza (not at the end), all the other end words from stanza one.

Here's Algernon Charles Swinburne's "Sestina":—

Ultimate Style

I saw my soul at rest upon a day
    As a bird sleeping in the nest of night,
   Among soft leaves that give the starlight way
     To touch its wings but not its eyes with light;
So that it knew as one in visions may,
    And knew not as men waking, of delight.

   This was the measure of my soul's delight;
    It had no power of joy to fly by day,
Nor part in the large lordship of the light;
   But in a secret moon-beholden way
Had all its will of dreams and pleasant night,
    And all the love and life that sleepers may.

But such life's triumph as men waking may
   It might not have to feed its faint delight
Between the stars by night and sun by day,
   Shut up with green leaves and a little light;
Because its way was as a lost star's way,
   A world's not wholly known of day or night.

All loves and dreams and sounds and gleams of night
   Made it all music that such minstrels may,
And all they had they gave it of delight;
   But in the full face of the fire of day
What place shall be for any starry light,
   What part of heaven in all the wide sun's way?

Yet the soul woke not, sleeping by the way,
　　Watched as a nursling of the large-eyed night,
And sought no strength nor knowledge of the day,
　　Nor closer touch conclusive of delight,
Nor mightier joy nor truer than dreamers may,
　　Nor more of song than they, nor more of light.

For who sleeps once and sees the secret light
　　Whereby sleep shows the soul a fairer way
Between the rise and rest of day and night,
　　Shall care no more to fare as all men may,
But be his place of pain or of delight,
　　There shall he dwell, beholding night as day.

Song, have thy day and take thy fill of light
　　Before the night be fallen across thy way;
Sing while he may, man hath no long delight.

Ultimate Style

Pantoum A pantoum can be any length, but it consists of four-line stanzas. The second and fourth lines of each stanza become the first and third lines of the next stanza, so each stanza is linked to the next. The last stanza repeats the first stanza's first and third lines. Take a look at this excerpt from John Ashbery's "Pantoum":

Eyes shining without mystery,
Footprints eager for the past
Through the vague snow of many clay pipes,
And what is in store?

Footprints eager for the past
The usual obtuse blanket.
And what is in store
For those dearest to the king?

Rondel, Rondeau, Roundel   Rondel, rondeau, and roundel are three different terms for what was originally a highly artificial French form. They are all similar—they all refer to a poem featuring repetition, with two rhymes only. The rondel (also known as the roundel) has fourteen lines, the rondeau thirteen or fifteen. The form varies quite a bit in terms of how many lines or parts of lines are repeated—when it's repeated, it's referred to as a refrain. Here's Algernon Charles Swinburne's "Rondel," from the mid-nineteenth century:

Kissing her hair I sat against her feet,
Wove and unwove it, wound and found it sweet;
Made fast therewith her hands, drew down her eyes,
Deep as deep flowers and dreamy like dim skies;
With her own tresses bound and found her fair,
    Kissing her hair.

Sleep were no sweeter than her face to me,
Sleep of cold sea-bloom under the cold sea;
What pain could get between my face and hers?
What new sweet thing would love not relish worse?
Unless, perhaps, white death had kissed me there,
    Kissing her hair?

Triolet   A triolet is an eight-line form that uses only two rhymes, and a rhyme scheme of ABaAabAB. The first line, A, is repeated in lines 4, and 7; the second line, B, is repeated in line 8. (Capital letters means the line is repeated.) The lowercase *a* and *b* share only the same rhyme as the uppercase letters. While such a short, tightly wrought form is more easily used for lighter verse, Thomas Hardy used it expertly to express grief in "How Great My Grief":

> How great my grief, my joys how few,
> Since first it was my fate to know thee!
> —Have the slow years not brought to view
> How great my grief, my joys how few,
> Nor memory shaped old times anew,
> > Nor loving-kindness helped to show thee
> How great my grief, my joys how few,
> > Since first it was my fate to know thee?

Ultimate Style

The Sonnet   The most well-known traditional form in poetry is the sonnet, a fourteen-line poem written in iambic pentameter. It's a popular form because it's lyrical and brief. There are three types:

- Petrarchan
- Shakespearean
- Spenserian (which is only slightly different from the Shakespearean)

The basic difference is the rhyme scheme, but the flow of thought, or the argument of the poem, also varies.

- **Petrarchan Sonnet:** The Italian, or Petrarchan, sonnet is split up into two parts, an octave (eight lines) and a sestet (six lines). The octave's rhyme scheme is ABBAABBA; the sestet's is open, though it always includes several rhymes. It sometimes, though not often, ends with a two-line rhyme, or couplet. A traditional sestet may be rhymed as CDCDCD or CDECDE. The significance of having an octave and then a sestet is in the turning point between the two. The first section sets up the argument or situation, and the next one develops it in some way. Take a look at the Petrarchan sonnet "Holy Sonnet XIV" by John Donne:

> Batter my heart, three-personed God; for, you
> As yet but knock, breathe, shine, and seek to mend;
> That I may rise, and stand, o'erthrow me, 'and bend
> Your force, to break, blow, burn and make me new.
> I, like an usurped town, to another due,
> Labour to admit you, but Oh, to no end;
> Reason your viceroy in me, me should defend,
> But is captived, and proves weak or untrue.
> Yet dearly I love you, and would be loved fain,
> But am betrothed unto your enemy:
> Divorce me, untie, or break that knot again;
> Take me to you, imprison me, for I,
> Except you enthrall me, never shall be free,
> Nor ever chaste, except you ravish me.

In this sonnet, Donne is questioning God with a fury. True of the Petrarchan form, there's a "turn" after the first eight lines. On the line that begins "Yet dearly I love you," the attitude changes. Instead of moaning about how he cannot admit God, he admits that he loves God, so he wants to admit him—but he can't. And then he continues to pour out his heart, confiding that he'll never be free and will always want to be in God's presence.

- **Shakespearean Sonnet:** In a Shakespearean sonnet, the rhyme scheme is ABABCDCDEFEFGG. The final two-line couplet is a kind of flourish, where you have to make a point or sum things up. Here's Shakespeare's "Sonnet 30":

> When to the sessions of sweet silent thought
> I summon up remembrance of things past,
> I sigh the lack of many a thing I sought,
> And with old woes new wail my dear time's waste:
> Then can I drown an eye, unused to flow,
> For precious friends hid in death's dateless night,
> And weep afresh love's long since cancelled woe,
> And moan the expense of many a vanished sight:
> Then can I grieve at grievances foregone,
> And heavily from woe to woe tell o'er
> The sad account of fore-bemoaned moan,
> Which I new pay as if not paid before.
> But if the while I think on thee, dear friend,
> All losses are restor'd and sorrows end.

One of Shakespeare's most beautiful and pensive poems, "Sonnet 30" deals with the speaker's reckoning of his life. He's lost a lot, lacked a lot, and feels like time has been wasted. But then he thinks about a friend who died, and the joy of thinking about him dissolves his sorrow and gives back to him what he wanted from his life.

- **Spenserian Sonnet:** The Spenserian sonnet rhymes as follows: ABABBCBCCDCDEE. The second four lines are linked by rhymes to the first four and to the following four, and a couplet concludes the poem by reemphasizing the main idea or proposing an alternate view. Here's Edmund Spenser's "Happy ye leaves! whenas those lily hands":

> Happy ye leaves! whenas those lily hands,
> Which hold my life in their dead doing might,
> Shall handle you, and hold in love's soft bands,
> Like captives trembling at the victor's sight.
> And happy lines! on which, with starry light,
> Those lamping eyes will deign sometimes to look,
> And read the sorrows of my dying sprite,
> Written with tears in heart's close bleeding book.
> And happy rhymes! bathed in the sacred brook
> Of Helicon, whence she derived is,
> When ye behold that angel's blessed look,
> My soul's long lacked food, my heaven's bliss.
> Leaves, lines, and rhymes seek her to please alone,
> Whom if ye please, I care for other none.

Sonnetlike Forms   Plenty of poets have taken the sonnet form and approximated it by using a different number of lines, a more casual tone of voice, and a different rhyme scheme. The point is that the fourteen-line sonnet still has some influence over the way the poem is written. A nineteen-line poem that works kind of like a sonnet, with occasional rhymes, is still closer in concept to a sonnet form than a long, bulky poem written like a paragraph or a poem consisting entirely of two-line couplets. You can use a sonnetlike form when you want to use a form but want some additional freedom too.

Ultimate Style

Change and Create Forms

After you write a poem, you should feel free to change its form. See how it reads in two-line stanzas. Is it working? Now see how it reads in three-line stanzas, or four-line stanzas. Or try using no stanzas at all. Which is better? Even if you slaved over a sonnet or a villanelle, you may eventually choose to loosen up the form and make it very different.

Most poets create their own forms. Marianne Moore wrote poems by counting syllables and making sure each line has the same number (a technique called *syllabic meter*). Here are the first two lines from a poem called "The Steeple-Jack":

> Dürer would have seen a reason for living
> in towns like this, with eight stranded whales

Counting syllables is more difficult than you might think: not everyone can write gracefully in a preset form like this.

Moore had to find the right word, with the right number of syllables, that made the right kind of sense. A scene, or group of thoughts, spans the rest of the stanza, but the lines themselves don't convey unique thoughts. Like Moore, you should experiment with your poems and find what works for you.

Express Wild Feelings

Sometimes it's easier to give intense feelings form when you *literally* give them form. When you're trying to write a poem that really touches an emotional nerve, you may find yourself with a poem that's chaotic, with little logic. *You* may understand the craziness, but it won't make for an effective poem because readers won't be able to connect to the wild emotions you've conveyed. A better way to convey wild emotions is to write a poem that reigns in the chaos through form. This is extremely difficult—but it will result in a more sophisticated poem.

You may think that if a poem is chaotic, it can serve as an accurate representation of your own chaotic feelings. But consider this: a wild poem gives your feelings too much space to run around. *Containing* those feelings—or trying to—in a form actually intensifies them. Think about anger, for example: the intensity builds as long as you keep the anger contained; if you let it out explosively, it loses its power. Your emotion will be conveyed through the form—readers will see that nothing really contains the chaos. When emotion bursts from a poem that at first glance looks orderly, it's all the more affecting.

Form in Action

W. H. Auden uses form to convey feelings of grief in
"Funeral Blues."

Funeral Blues

Stop all the clocks, cut off the telephone,
Prevent the dog from barking with a juicy bone,
Silence the pianos and with muffled drum
Bring out the coffin, let the mourners come.

Let aeroplanes circle moaning overhead
Scribbling on the sky the message He is Dead.
Put crepe bows round the white necks of the public doves,
Let the traffic policemen wear black cotton gloves.

He was my North, my South, my East and West,
My working week and my Sunday rest,
My noon, my midnight, my talk, my song;
I thought that love would last forever: I was wrong.

The stars are not wanted now; put out every one,
Pack up the moon and dismantle the sun,
Pour away the ocean and sweep up the wood;
For nothing now can ever come to any good.

Auden organizes this poem into quatrains, end-rhyming the
first two and the last two lines of each, and this tight form
helps him convey deep emotions. The speaker in this poem is
heartbroken: someone close to him has died. He never comes
out and says "I am heartbroken," but he gives evidence of the

heartbreak. He wants the world to change: for the clocks to stop, even for the moon and sun to disappear. He thinks the whole world should suffer this loss, that the death should be written across the sky and that no good can ever again be possible. He never says, "I loved this person deeply"—but he makes those feelings perfectly clear in the third stanza, when he names all the things this person is to him.

This poem, with its extreme grief and sadness, could easily have been overly sentimental, even off-putting. But form gives structure and organization to the emotional wildness inside the poem. The speaker's heartbreak is given shape through form.

Exercises

- Create your own near-sonnet form. You can vary the rhyme scheme and the length of the stanzas, but try to keep some element of the sonnet.

- Write a short poem in which every line has the same number of syllables. Then revise the poem, loosening up the form if necessary to get the effect you want.

- Find a poem you like that's written in free verse and put it into form. You can include rhyme or choose not to include it, but think carefully about which form is most suitable. Once you've written a draft, revise the poem to better fit into the form you chose.

Free Verse

T. S. Eliot, author of one of the twentieth century's most representative poems, "The Waste Land," famously said in a 1917 essay that free verse "is a battle-cry of freedom, and there is no freedom in art." He concludes: "there is only good verse, bad verse, and chaos." But guess what: Eliot himself wrote free verse. So what did he mean?

Basically, Eliot meant that free verse shouldn't be considered sloppy or easy poetry. Free verse is poetry without form, written without rhyme or meter—but it requires the same kind of attention to detail in order to work well. Free verse is *not* just carelessly written verse. It succeeds when it carefully evades or approximates patterns. (Know the rules first, then break them.) Free verse won't be effective if you simply spew words onto the page haphazardly. Today, free verse is the norm, and the poets who succeed tend to be those who have studied technique and mastered it before moving on to free verse.

9

Be Creative, Not Careless

You may assume that formal verse is more difficult than free verse. In formal verse, you have to count out syllables, monitor rhythm, and find rhymes—all while keeping your syntax and ideas interesting. Meanwhile, with free verse, you can just write off the top of your head. Right? Not so fast.

Imagine someone sits you down at a piano and asks you to improvise a brand-new version of "Piano Man." If you've been playing "Piano Man" for years, you're in luck: the formal version is so familiar to you that it's easy to come up with jazzy changes. If you've never played "Piano Man" in your life, you're lost: you don't even know the original chords, let alone how to riff on them. It's a complete guessing game, and your attempt isn't pretty. The same problem arises if you try to write free verse with *no* background in form. You end up in a guessing game, writing however you please, with no clear influence or motivation. That's not creative—that's careless.

Ultimate Style

Free verse is not free association, and it's not just lines cut up into pieces and thrown down on the page. Good free verse takes skill and practice.

The Urge to Cheat Too often, young writers think free verse gives them free reign to call a few dashed-off lines "poetry." But experienced poets know that it takes a lot of effort to look effortless. Even short poems with few words require careful thought, evaluation, and revision to ensure that each word is the *right* word and that the sound, rhythm, and effect of the poem are exactly how you want them to be. It's too easy to cheat or pretend that you're doing something bold when you're really just avoiding the work of writing a good poem.

Be Deliberately Free

Even though you may find yourself writing in free verse
naturally, you should take a moment to consider why you're
choosing free verse rather than a form. What can free verse
convey that a form cannot? You may have more of a feeling
about it than a concrete, academic answer, and that's fine.
The point is to *be deliberate* when you're deciding how to go
about writing a poem. Don't let free verse be your fallback just
because it's the contemporary norm. If you pay attention to
your structure, you'll be better able to maximize the effectiveness of every aspect of your poem.

Use Sound

You can make free verse musical by paying close attention to
sound. Even when you're not rhyming, you should make sure
your words connect to each other and that the lines of your
poem flow. Free verse can have a music all its own.

Take a look at these two lines from Walt Whitman's poem
"Song of Myself":

> I loafe and invite my soul,
> I lean and loafe at my ease observing a spear of summer
> grass.

There's no rhyme scheme and no meter, but his lines are
exactingly crafted. Whitman employs a great deal of poetic
technique, particularly with sound. He uses assonance: *lean*

and *ease* and *spear*, *loafe* and *soul*. He also uses consonance: *lean/loafe*, *spear/summer*, and even the *s* sounds in *ease*, *observing*, and *grass*. He also deliberately repeats *loafe* for added rhythm and music. This is free verse, but Whitman has chosen every word carefully to give these lines their music.

Make Lines Matter

Free verse relies on careful line structure to come alive. Far from being "free," lines in a free-verse poem must be structured carefully, and you should pay close attention to how each line relates to the next. Without rhyme or meter to link lines, structure is key in writing a tight, coherent poem.

Ultimate Style

In the poem "Florida," Elizabeth Bishop uses syntax to create a well-formed poem, as shown in the first four lines:

> The state with the prettiest name,
> The state that floats in brackish water,
> Held together by mangrove roots
> That bear while living oysters in clusters,

Far from being haphazard, every line of this poem has been written with care. Bishop uses repetition in the first two lines: both begin with "The state." Each line is roughly the length of a breath. Bishop doesn't break the poem up into sentences, and each line connects easily to the next, like one long, drawn-out thought. She has considered word choice and syntax carefully. For example, "That bear while living oysters in clusters" is much more rhythmic than if she'd written "That support clusters of oysters." Bishop has also used concrete, vivid imagery. This free-verse poem required careful attention to poetic technique.

Line Breaks When you're writing free verse, you'll have to use careful judgment when deciding where to break your lines. Take a look at how carefully Bishop breaks lines in the previous excerpt from "Florida." The lines are concise, carefully formed, and approximately the same length. The line breaks are thoughtful and equivalent to a breath, and they require readers to pause naturally and frequently, slowing down the pace of the poem. The first and third lines end with one-syllable words, while the second and third lines end with two-syllable words. In this way, Bishop has connected the lines rhythmically, rather than breaking them randomly.

Blur Prose and Poetry

Is it prose, or is it poetry? Sometimes it's difficult to determine where to draw the line. A poem is usually easy to recognize, with line breaks and stanzas. But sometimes a very, very short story or a lyrical reflection, which ordinarily would be considered prose, can be considered a kind of poetry: a prose poem. A **prose poem** is simply a combination of a poem and a very short story or reflection. As in regular poetry, diction, syntax, rhythm, imagery, sound, pace, and figurative language are all of prime importance. A story may be there, but in a way the story itself is of secondary importance to the *way* the story is told. The parameters for what may be considered a prose poem are wide, and a lot of very beautiful writing may fall into this category.

Take a look at this prose poem, "Ruts," from Rimbaud's *Illuminations* (translated by Wyatt Mason):

> On the right, the summer dawn stirs the leaves and mists and noises of this corner of the park, while on the left, embankments keep the wet road's thousand little ruts in violet shadow. A stream of enchantments: Wagons filled with gilded animals, poles, and motley tenting, drawn at full gallop by twenty dappled circus horses, and children and men riding amazing beasts: twenty gilded conveyances, flagged and flowered like ancient coaches, like something from a fairy tale, filled with children dressed for a country fair. There are even coffins, sporting ebony plumes, beneath night-dark canopies, behind the trot of massive blue-black mares.

Ultimate Style

Rimbaud didn't just observe what was around him and write it down, and this prose poem isn't really about ruts. He's employed vibrant, varied imagery, alliteration, and careful diction. The poem is full of beautiful phrases, such as "embankments keep the wet road's thousand little ruts in violet shadow"—though it's written in paragraph form, the language is undeniably poetic. Phrases such as the "stream of enchantments" are evocative and unusual. The sentences are concise, unsentimental, and bold, and each is vital to the work, just as each line is vital to a poem. In "Ruts," Rimbaud has created both a poem and a story—a prose poem.

Free Verse in Action

Walt Whitman was America's great free versifier, as exemplified here in a poem called "Broadway":

Broadway

What hurrying human tides, or day or night!

What passions, winnings, losses, ardours, swim thy waters!

What whirls of evil, bliss and sorrow, stem thee!

What curious questioning glances—glints of love!

Leer, envy, scorn, contempt, hope, aspiration!

Thou portal—thou arena—thou of the myriad long-drawn
    Lines and groups!

(Could but thy flagstones, curbs, facades, tell their
    inimitable tales;

Thy windows rich, and huge hotels—thy side-walks wide;)

Thou of the endless sliding, mincing, shuffling feet!

Thou, like the parti-colored world itself—like infinite,
    Teeming, mocking life!

Thou visor'd, vast, unspeakable show and lesson!

Whitman wrote in free verse, but he was ruthless in how carefully he constructed his poems. Here, he starts by using repetition for the first four lines, a repetition that becomes almost like a chant. We get the sense of how awed he is by the city life he sees around him—he can't point things out fast enough. Those first four lines anchor us in the scene. He goes on to list more specific details, but he begins going deeper into those details and inserting his thoughts and questions about them.

What kind of stories would the sidewalks tell? What "lesson" is he referring to in the final line? We feel almost battered by images and details, and the free-verse form of the poem gives Whitman enough space to create this sense of chaos, busyness, and liveliness. City life isn't something you can easily contain, so the sprawling free-verse form is appropriate.

Exercises

- Write a Whitmanesque poem in which you describe in free verse something chaotic that can't be contained—it can be a place, a feeling, a person, or anything else you can think of.

- Write a short poem in free verse in which you make every line as musical as possible. Think about the sound of every word.

- Write a 100-word prose poem about your day. Excise any extra words, and keep it as tight as possible. Make your description vivid and poetic.

Meter

Meter is a pattern of stressed syllables that helps organize your poem. When a syllable is *stressed*, it means there's emphasis on that syllable. For example, in the word *country*, the first syllable is stressed: COUNtry. In the word *affair*, the second syllable is stressed: afFAIR. Arranging stresses logically in a line of poetry creates meter.

Learning about meter can bring you great rewards. Once you understand the technical aspects of a poem, you'll be better equipped to understand the poem's wit, irony, and meaning. And by practicing meter, you'll become an expert at navigating rhythms. Learning meter will help you write better poetry: you'll be more in tune with structure and rhythm, and you'll be able to identify problem areas in your poems. When you have a handle on meter, you may be surprised to discover that much of your free verse flirts with metered patterns—even when you don't do it consciously. Your poems will be more sophisticated when you have knowledge and technical skill behind them.

10

Learn the Units

The smallest unit of a poem is a syllable. There are two kinds of syllables: stressed and unstressed. After the syllable, the next largest unit is the **foot**, which is a group of two or more stressed and unstressed syllables. There are five types of feet, and each has its own number of syllables:

1. *Iamb*: two syllables
2. *Trochee*: two syllables
3. *Spondee*: two syllables
4. *Pyrrhic*: two syllables
5. *Anapest*: three syllables
6. *Dactyl*: three syllables

The difference among these five types of feet is where the stresses fall. In the world of poetry, a stressed syllable is marked as a /, and an unstressed syllable is marked as a U.

Ultimate Style

1. Iamb: an unstressed syllable followed by a stressed syllable (U /)
   * Today, unless, unseen, correct, around, create, complete

2. Trochee: a stressed syllable followed by an unstressed syllable (/ U)
   * Bookish, towel, factoid, pencil, paper, finger, picture

3. Spondee: two stressed syllables, one after the other (/ /)
   * Hot food, lifelong, shipshape, street-smart, look sharp

4. Pyrrhic: two unstressed syllables, one after the other (U U)
   * And the, of the, understand (the *under* is the pyrrhic)

5. Anapest: two unstressed syllables followed by a stressed syllable (U U /)
   * Understand, interact, unabridged, in a tree

6. Dactyl: a stressed syllable followed by two unstressed syllables (/ U U)

- Telephone, temperament, quietly, musical, alphabet, rotating

Identify Meter

To determine the meter of a poem, you must first identify the type of foot being used, then count how many feet appear in each line:

- *Monometer*: one foot
- *Dimeter*: two feet
- *Trimeter*: three feet
- *Tetrameter*: four feet
- *Pentameter*: five feet
- *Hexameter*: six feet

This list is endless: you can keep going up to as many feet as you can fit on a line. However, you likely won't be using more than six feet, unless you're writing *extremely* long sentences.

Type + Number = Meter   Monometer, dimeter, and so forth are just half of what's considered the meter of a poem. The name for the type of meter includes the *type* of foot being used along with the *number* of feet. For example, look at this one-word line:

Station

Station is a trochee, because it's a stressed syllable followed by an unstressed syllable: STAtion. Since there is only one trochee (one foot) on this line, it's a monometer. What you have here is *trochaic monometer* (*troachaic* is the adjective form of *trochee*).

Now look at this line:

I walked the streets and looked for something new

First, you must figure out what kind of foot is being used. Read the line out loud: some syllables are stressed, and others aren't. Mark up the line as you read it:

Ultimate Style

U / U / U / U / U /
I walked the streets and looked for something new

There's a pattern of U / , which should look familiar: it's an iamb. And there are five iambs in the line. The meter here is, therefore, *iambic pentameter*, one of the most common meters in poetry.

Scanning Reading a poem, marking stressed and unstressed syllables, and identifying its meter is called scanning a poem, or scansion. Scanning isn't always easy. Not all lines have easy-to-identify feet, and sometimes you have to go by instinct. Read the words out loud, as though you're in normal conversation—don't try to sound grand or "poetic." You're more likely to get the stresses right if you read normally.

If you scan several lines, you'll start seeing a pattern, and you'll have discovered the meter of the poem. Remember that not all poems have meter—often, free verse is written without a set meter, or it may consist of a combination of different meters. Scanning is still useful, however. It can show you how carefully a poet has constructed a poem and help you understand how the poet has created tension and emotion.

Substitutions   Take a look at the first two lines from "Song" by John Donne. Read them out loud and mark the stresses:

> / /   / U / U /
> Sweetest love, I do not goe,

> U / U / U /
> For weariness of thee,

Take a close look at the feet in the second line: there are three iambs (U /) in a row, so we know we're dealing with iambic trimeter. But look at the first word of the poem: *Sweetest* is a spondee (/ /), followed by the second half of an iamb (/) and then two full iambs (U /). This line is considered *iambic trimeter*, even though the first foot isn't technically an iamb. Using a spondee in a line otherwise full of iambs is called a substitution. Meter involves more than just filling out the line with the exact foot and keeping everything consistent and exact. You can substitute feet here and there, and those substitutions are often what keep a poem exciting. In this case, the forceful beginning puts the emphasis on the person Donne is addressing, *Sweetest love*, and pulls you into the poem.

Know the Tones

When you write, you should choose the type of foot you use deliberately, because each type of foot creates a different tone. When you work with a poem or even just a line or two, you can choose the type of foot to create the effect you want.

Ultimate Style

Iambs Iambs are natural and conversational. Take a look at the following sentence:

> I went to sleep and dreamed about a fish.

Iambs are the mainstay of the English language, and most groups of words fall into iambs naturally. It's no accident that historically, the majority of poetry in English is in unrhymed iambic pentameter (called *blank verse*). So if you're writing in meter, most likely you'll find your lines naturally falling into an iambic pattern. To do anything else, you'll have to work at it.

Trochees Trochees are strong and brash. Take a look at a line from John Donne's "Holy Sonnet XIV":

> Batter my heart, three-personed God; for, you

The trochee, *batter*, is aggressive and violent. That same effect couldn't be achieved with an iamb or an anapest.

Spondees   Spondees are dramatic. They get your attention: "Stop there!" Look at how Keats uses a spondee in his "Ode on a Grecian Urn":

> Thou still unravish'd bride of quietness,
>   Thou foster-child of silence and slow time.

The spondee, "slow time," is literally *slow time*. It's a spondee, with two accented syllables next to each other, which slows the line down. The lines preceding the spondee are in iambic pentameter, so the substitution, a break in the flow, really hits home. But again, you can't write an entire poem of spondees. It might read something like this:

> Don't wait! Fall fast, oak tree. Break hard right now,
> Crack, burn–down, down. Time waits, force-free, for you.

That sounds ridiculous. You're forced to use monosyllabic words, which limits you, and it's difficult to piece together a sentence that makes sense.

Pyrrhics   Pyrrhics, with their unstressed syllables, create a tone of sadness and loss. Keats uses a pyrrhic at the end of a line in his poem "La Belle Dame sans Merci":

> Alone and palely loitering

By ending the line with a pyrrhic (the second two syllables of *loitering* form the pyrrhic), Keats trails off thoughtfully and sadly.

Anapests   Anapests are lively, light, and speedy. They move fast:

Swinging up to the trees

Those are two anapests in a row: swinging UP to the TREES. Anapests are not dramatic, and you wouldn't compose an entire poem out of them. Instead, you'd substitute them into the existing meter to make a point or create an effect.

Ultimate Style

Dactyls   You likely won't encounter dactyls very often, except in substitutions. Dactyls—dactylic hexameter in particular—are, traditionally, a Greek and Latin classical meter. Homer wrote epics in dactyls—but the Greek language is more conducive to dactyls than the English language. Technically, you can you write an entire poem of dactyls, but it would sound pretty weird. The nineteenth-century poet Henry Wadsworth Longfellow tried his hand at dactylic hexameter in English, in his poem "Evangeline":

This is the forest primeval. The murmuring pines and the hemlocks

It starts off fine, with a pleasing rhythm. Now here's an excerpt from a later part of the poem:

> Sat in his elbow-chair; and watched how the flames and the
> smoke-wreaths
> Struggled together like foes in a burning city. Behind him,
> Nodding and mocking along the wall, with gestures fantastic,
> Darted his own huge shadow, and vanished away into darkness.
> Faces, clumsily carved in oak, on the back of his arm-chair
> Laughed in the flickering light, and the pewter plates on the
> dresser
> Caught and reflected the flame, as shields of armies the
> sunshine.
> Fragments of song the old man sang, and carols of Christmas,
> Such as at home, in the olden time, his fathers before him
> Sang in their Norman orchards and bright Burgundian vineyards.

It's peppered with dactyls but isn't quite in dactylic hexameter. Nonetheless, you can see how the form enforces a kind of forward motion. The same or similar rhythm courses through, line after line, and makes it start to sound awkward and even dull. Every line begins with a stressed syllable, which gets repetitive quickly.

Dactyls are forceful here and there, but in English, when constructing an entire poem out of them, you're almost certain to write something that falls short of what you intended.

Be Flexible

As you write, you might find that it's easier to write intuitively, and what shows up on the page will reveal your preferences and talents. Even without focusing on meter, you may find that you naturally fall into certain patterns. Some poets tend to write lines with about five accents, such as traditional iambic pentameter, and others write shorter lines with fewer accents. Do what feels right to you. When you do consider meter, be flexible. You can always add meter, remove the meter, shorten the lines, lengthen the lines, and add substitutions. Most important, sticking rigidly to a meter is not a sign of technical skill—it's a sign of rigidity. Losing the pattern for a few feet, or just obeying the pattern loosely, is perfectly fine.

The Crutch of Meter   Meter can be a crutch: you may think you can write a solid poem just by filling in the meter. However, such thoughtlessness will result in a nursery rhyme, not a good poem. A good rule of thumb: if your poem sounds too cute, you know you've paid more attention to meter than to the phrasing and flow of your poem.

Ultimate Style

Read the Poem, Not the Meter

When you read a poem that's written in meter, read the poem, not the meter. In other words, don't read it like a nursery rhyme and pause at the end of the line just *because* it's the end of the line. Doing so will lead you to butcher a beautiful, lyrical poem and make it sound like a sputtering engine. Instead, read the poem as if the meter weren't there. Read it as though you're speaking normally, as though you're reading sentences, not lines. This will make you a much more affecting reader, and people will stop and listen.

Meter in Action

Meter was an underlying structure for Yeats's rhythms, not the main point, and in "The Cold Heaven," he freely uses substitutions rather than sticking rigidly to meter.

The Cold Heaven

Suddenly I saw the cold and rook-delighting Heaven

That seemed as though ice burned and was but the more ice,

And thereupon imagination and heart were driven

So wild that every casual thought of that and this

Vanished, and left but memories, that should be out of season

With the hot blood of youth, of love crossed long ago;

And I took all the blame out of all sense and reason,

Until I cried and trembled and rocked to and fro,

Riddled with light. Ah! when the ghost begins to quicken,

Confusion of the death-bed over, is it sent

Out naked on the roads, as the books say, and stricken

By the injustice of the skies for punishment?

Right away we have a dactyl, *suddenly*, before the basic iambic hexameter line begins. In line 2, we have two iambic feet, "that seemed as though," followed by another substitution, the spondee "ice burned." Yeats doesn't lose a step: he slides right back into his iambic pattern. But try to follow the meter throughout the entire poem—you can't. There's one substitution after another—spondees, dactyls, anapests—and the lines swing from six feet to seven and back to six.

The great thing about meter is that it can be varied and loose. This outstanding poem uses the fundamentals of meter but in an instinctive and rhythmic way. Yeats veers away from the meter more than he sticks to it, but you can still see that he has command over the technique. Look at how the last line, written in perfect iambic hexameter, concludes not with a statement but with a question. That's the brilliance of Yeats and the brilliance of an expert metrist: within a perfectly formed, exactingly produced, tight metrical line is an open-ended question.

Ultimate Style

Exercises

- Write a four-line stanza, using the following meters in any order: iambic pentameter, iambic quadrameter, iambic trimeter, and iambic dimeter.

- Make a list of the standard feet (iamb, trochee, etc.) and write down as many words (or phrases) as you can think of for each.

- Write a short poem adhering strictly to iambic pentameter. Then revise the poem, loosening up the meter and adding substitutions to create greater emotion and effect.

Rhythm

You already know what rhythm is on a basic level—it's what makes music memorable or songs catchy. It's what you have (or don't have) when you dance. Poems have rhythm too: it's the music of a poem. Without rhythm, you have no poem, only thoughtful or compelling phrases written down, with line breaks, on a page. Rhythm connects those lines together and makes the whole poem larger than the sum of its parts. Rhythm incorporates nearly every other poetic concept: rhyme, meter, sound, diction and syntax, even imagery.

Rhythm is created from a few basic components: repetition, pacing, the sounds in words, and verbs. When you learn to identify each of these components in a poem, you'll start getting a sense of why some poems have rhythm and others don't. Rhythm is the most difficult part of poetry to grasp, and only by reading lots of poems, and experimenting with your own, will you gain a thorough understanding of it.

11

Repeat, Repeat

Songs are built on repetition, and repetition helps us learn. We tend to remember a chorus of a song better than the other words, simply because we hear it more often and because it provides a basic melody or beat around which the rest of the song revolves. Using repetition is a surefire way to get people to remember what you have to say, and it can give your poem a unique rhythm. But repetition means more than just flat-out repeating lines or words. You should *vary* the rhythm to make your poem musical and memorable.

Take a look at how William Wordsworth repeats the word *five* in his famous poem, "Lines Composed a Few Miles above Tintern Abbey, On Revisiting the Banks of the Wye during a Tour. July 13, 1798":

> Five years have passed; five summers, with the length
> Of five long winters! and again I hear
> These waters, rolling from their mountain-springs
> With a soft inland murmur.

Ultimate Style

Read it out loud, then reread it without the first *five*. Read it again without the first *or* last *five*. The effects are very different. The word *five* not only ties the other words together but also forces you to feel the heaviness of those years. Notice how Wordsworth used the word *five* in varying places—he didn't start every line with the same word. He varied his repetition so the *five* really breaks up the lines of the poem. The plodding rhythm of five … five … five … stretches out the pace of the poem.

Elizabeth Bishop uses repetition masterfully to create rhythm in these lines from "At the Fishhouses":

> I have seen it over and over, the same sea, the same,
> slightly, indifferently swinging above the stones,
> icily free above the stones,
> above the stones and then the world.

Here, almost every word is repeated. *Over* and *same* are used twice, and *stones* and *above* appear three times. All this is tightly packed into just a few lines. But Bishop does more: she uses similar *sounds* repetitively as well. The word *sea* in the first line rhymes with *free* in the third line. And she repeats sounds in three adverbs: *slightly, indifferently,* and *icily.* Plus, in this short section, there are ten instances of alliteration with the letter *S*.

That's not all. In the first line, the rhythm is singsongy and moves fast, but by the second line, it quickly changes and becomes more forceful. The rhythm of this poem varies and builds to create a swaying, sealike rhythm.

Pace Your Poem

You've heard the phrase "pace yourself" plenty of times: it relates to energy. Rhythm is related to energy too. Just as energy courses through a marathon runner's body, rhythm courses through a poem, driving it forward. Rhythm moves through, or across, a line or sentence. The words themselves don't have rhythm, but when they are connected together in certain ways, rhythm appears. The deliberate pacing of this energy creates rhythm.

Imagine reading line after line of poetry at the same speed: it gets monotonous. Now imagine that each sentence is identical in structure:

The sparrow flew over the trees
And settled on a branch.

A ladybug crawled up my arm
And waited on my shoulder.

You'd be hard-pressed to write a more monotonous poem. The pacing is too regular, too similar, and too dull. There is no variation and very little energy. To improve the rhythm of your poems, keep in mind the length of each sentence and how fast each sentence is moving.

Take a look at Samuel Taylor Coleridge's expert pacing in "Frost at Midnight":

Ultimate Style

The frost performs its secret ministry
Unhelped by any wind. The owlet's cry
Came loud—and hark, again! loud as before.
The inmates of my cottage, all at rest,
Have left me to that solitude, which soothes
Abstruser musings: save that at my side
My cradled infant slumbers peacefully.
'Tis calm indeed!

The poem is written in iambic pentameter, which contributes to the flow of the first line. It's a soft line, with lots of s sounds, and it moves with ease. The second line is in the same meter, but there's a caesura (pause) in the middle: this breaks the continuity momentarily, before the pace picks up again. In the third line, Coleridge takes action, strongly emphasizing the words *loud*, *hark*, and *again*. It's still in iambic pentameter, but the trick is in how he shatters the pace abruptly, three times in a row. He then picks up the pace again, dragging out the sentence over five lines. When you get to "'Tis calm indeed!" you're ready for a change. The exclamation stops the flow, which makes the poem more exciting.

Coleridge also manipulates line breaks to create rhythm. The poem starts with one sentence over one and a half lines. Then we get almost one sentence per line. Then, on line 3, the phrase "loud as before" takes up only half a line. After all that, Coleridge settles down in one sentence for four full lines before inserting another sentence in half a line. Rhythm appears through this sort of back-and-forth. Coleridge stays true to the meter while still enlivening the sentences with pauses and brief exclamatory sentences, and the result is an energetic, rhythmic poem that still manages to sound quiet, even private.

Make Words Count

Every word in a poem plays a role in creating rhythm. You use words to portray a subject, but the subject itself is only *part* of a poem. Sometimes the words themselves affect the poem in a way that has nothing to do with the *meaning* of the words: sometimes you can use words to *imitate* the subject.

Take a look at "A Noiseless Patient Spider" by Walt Whitman:

> A noiseless patient spider,
> I mark'd where on a little promontory it stood isolated,
> Mark'd how to explore the vacant vast surrounding,
> It launch'd forth filament, filament, filament, out of itself,
> Ever unreeling them, ever tirelessly speeding them.

Whitman not only describes the spider but, in the fourth and fifth lines, he also *imitates* it with words. He uses the repetition of *filament* to show the spider's thread getting longer and longer—the words even connect together in a kind of chain. Notice the repetition of the long *e* sounds in the fifth line, and how, when you say the line out loud, the words themselves sound like they're the threads being unspooled by the spider. *Unreeling* and *speeding* even look like thin threads, and the rhythm of the words makes you pause slightly on the *ee* in each one. Whitman not only tells you about this spider, but he actually uses words that are spiderlike.

Ultimate Style

Look how different the line would be if Whitman had written the fifth line this way:

Ever producing more and more lengths of thread in the air.

Read it out loud—it doesn't sound like a spider's thin filaments, and we don't get that wonderful, spidery *ee* sound. Plus, there are more words. All those extra words drag the line down, making it sound less like poetry and more like prose. Remember this as you write. A few extra words, an accent here instead of there, a word that doesn't sound right—all of this changes the rhythm of your poem. Details matter.

Not every poem imitates its subject through the diction (words) or syntax (the way the sentence flows). Some poems are simply descriptive and can be compelling as stories are compelling; other poems care more for form and sound than for actual meaning. The best poets use a blend of both approaches. They say something relevant, and they do it skillfully by organizing words in interesting ways and using words that sound exciting or abrupt.

Use Action Verbs

Rhythm is all about movement, so action verbs—verbs that really move—are vital to creating a rhythmic poem. Strong verbs propel your sentences forward and create vibrant movement. An action verb is a verb that indicates an actual, physical movement (*run, scream, kiss*) rather than a state of being (*is, was, seems*). Using action verbs makes your writing lively, concrete, and vivid.

Take a look at this excerpt from Jonathan Swift's "A Description of a City Shower":

> A coming shower your shooting corns presage,
> Old aches throb, your hollow tooth will rage.
> Sauntering in coffeehouse is Dulman seen;
> He damns the climate and complains of spleen.

Swift uses many action verbs throughout these lines to enhance the poem's rhythm. Pain *presages* the storm, aches *throb*, a hollow tooth *rages*; and the person mentioned in the poem ("Dulman" is similar to saying "Smith"—it signifies an everyman) *damns* and *complains*. The rapid piling up of actions seems to mimic the forceful sounds of a rainstorm, in which falling rain is itself a piling up of sounds and actions. The verbs also make the lines and images vivid. We can *feel* the approach of this rainstorm, and we can almost see and hear the mutterings of people seeking refuge in a coffeehouse. The verbs add rhythm by making this poem active and exciting.

Rhythm in Action

Alfred Lord Tennyson uses a variety of techniques to create a lively, effective rhythm in this section of his long poem, *In Memoriam* A. H. H. written in 1850.

Ultimate Style

> Dark house, by which once more I stand
>   Here in the long unlovely street.
>   Doors, where my heart was used to beat
> So quickly, waiting for a hand.
>
> A hand that can be clasped no more
>   Behold me, for I cannot sleep,
>   And like a guilty thing I creep
> At earliest morning to the door.
>
> He is not here; but far away
>   The noise of life begins again,
>   And ghastly thro the drizzling rain
> On the bald street breaks the blank day.

Immediately Tennyson starts with two stressed syllables, *dark house*, which slows the pace and gives the beginning weight. By line 3, he again puts weight on the initial syllable, *doors*. And by doing it again in line 4, with two stressed syllables (*So* and the first syllable of *quickly*), the rhythm is established: forceful, varied, exciting.

In the second stanza, he uses iambic verse, which is lively and easy to read. Because it's iambic quadrameter, not pentameter, it reads faster, simply because there are fewer feet. Tennyson doesn't want to batter the reader with only strong syllables; he wants to create a flow, punctuated by drama in appropriate places. The sentences are enlivened with internal rhymes. The rhythm makes you move forward to catch the rhymes, and you pause when you find them—then press forward again.

The same rhythm continues in the third stanza. In the final few lines, the rhythm seems about to change again. The words *noise, ghastly,* and *drizzling* all allude to it in a subtle way, both by the violence and action in the meanings of the words and by the hard, rough sounds of the syllables inside the words. Finally, we get the forceful, vital observation: "On the bald street breaks the blank day." The meter is stripped away, not unlike how the heartbeat of Tennyson's friend was, in a sense, stripped away. The five strong beats here—with three explosive *b* sounds—feel urgent. The street and day are both empty, and *still* the sun breaks. It feels tragic. There are many similar, but slightly different, vowel sounds inside those stressed words, which is key to the keeping the rhythm lively. You're forced to read that line carefully, moving your mouth constantly to form the different sounds. This gives each sound, and that final action of the sun breaking, more weight. The similarity of the linked vowel sounds and the battering *b* sounds rush the line forward, but the complexity of all those sounds together slow the pace. The resulting rhythm, in that one last sentence, is fiery but sad, fast but serious.

Exercises

- Write a few lines of a poem, varying the rhythm in each line by using repetition, word choice, verbs, and line length.

- Take a look at this stanza from Keats's famous "Ode to a Nightingale" and note where he inserts action verbs and pauses one after another, and how after more abrupt, stop-and-start phrasing, the sentences tend to get faster and smoother. Note, also, how after a number of long sentences he inserts a quick-moving, short sentence, such as "And leaden-eyed despairs." Take the form, with its accents, pauses, and verbs, and imitate it by rewriting the stanza using your own phrasing.

Ultimate Style

Fade far away, dissolve, and quite forget
What thou among the leaves hast never known,
The weariness, the fever, and the fret
Here, where men sit and hear each other groan;
Where palsy shakes a few, sad, last grey hairs,
Where youth grows pale, and spectre-thin, and dies;
Where but to think is to be full of sorrow
And leaden-eyed despairs;
Where Beauty cannot keep her lustrous eyes,
Or new Love pine at them beyond tomorrow.

- Write a few lines that describe things you'd find in a city, such as traffic, crowds, street music, and subways, using words that imitate what you're describing. Focus on conveying the rhythm of city life.

Tone

In poetry, as in everyday conversation, your tone reflects your feelings. When you talk, you convey your tone unconsciously through what words you use, how loudly or forcefully you say them, and how fast you speak. The tone you use when you're elated is very different from the tone you use when you're heartbroken. Sometimes, tone transcends your best efforts to mask your true feelings: "I can hear it in the tone of your voice," someone might say if you're faking happiness. Tone tells all.

12

In a poem, tone is often just as subtle and unconscious—and also just as pervasive. Tone is the *attitude* of the poem. It's not something you add in after your poem is written. Rather, tone comes through your line length, punctuation, language, rhythm, and sounds. Each of these things contributes, in its own way, to the tone of your poem. Reading a lot of poetry and figuring out how tone is created will help you analyze how you can create and control tone in your own work. You should be aware of how all the elements of your poem add up so that the tone you've created is actually the tone you want.

Assume Nothing

A poem can have virtually any kind of tone—ironic, sad, nostalgic, angry, bitter, joyful, proud, nervous, loving, worshipful, eager, hopeful, or defeated. And these tones can appear in any type of poem. Don't assume that certain styles or forms always embody a particular tone. For example, a poem written in quatrains may appear serious and conservative, but inside those lines may be violent, sudden twists, exclamatory phrases, or silly diction. Similarly, a poem with a careful rhyme scheme may seem old-fashioned and sedate, but inside those rhymes may be moody, crazy feelings. Think of it this way: form is just a container for feeling. The words and the way you say them are what create the tone.

Convey Anger, Aggression, or Passion

Ultimate Style

Exclamations, short stop-and-start phrases, rambling lists, and coarse or physical diction—words like *blurb* or *whack*—create an aggressive, angry, or passionate tone. Anytime the line is broken repeatedly or suddenly, the tone gets violent. Take a look at this excerpt from Allen Ginsberg's "Howl":

> Moloch! Solitude! Filth! Ugliness! Ashcans and unobtainable
> dollars! Chil-
> dren screaming under the stairways! Boys sobbing in armies!
> Old
> men weeping in the parks!

Notice the identifying marks: exclamation points; abbreviated, fragmented phrases; a list; rough-sounding words; and a hyphenated word that suggests that the speaker is so vehement that he can't slow down long enough to install a line break. Now look at what Ginsberg is saying: dollars are unobtainable, and everyone is screaming, sobbing, and weeping. He feels outrage and frustration. There's no hope or clarity, only horror. If he had written a poem with shorter lines and longer phrases, he wouldn't be conveying such an aggressive tone. When you write in a stop-and-start style as Ginsberg does here, you suggest there's something difficult at stake, something so troubling that the writing cannot be smooth.

If you want to write in form, such as a sonnet, you can still convey an angry, aggressive, or passionate tone. Ginsberg's short, piled-up phrases and unstructured lines are an overt reflection of a disturbed state of mind, but any form can convey the same sort of tone. John Donne did so with terse phrases and a series of lists in his "Holy Sonnet XIV":

> Batter my heart, three-personed God; for, you
> As yet but knock, breathe, shine, and seek to mend;
> That I may rise, and stand, o'erthrow me, 'and bend
> Your force, to break, blow, burn and make me new.
> I, like an usurped town, to another due,
> Labour to admit you, but Oh, to no end,
> Reason your viceroy in me, me should defend,
> But is captived, and proves weak or untrue.
> Yet dearly I love you, and would be loved fain,
> But am betrothed unto your enemy:
> Divorce me, untie, or break that knot again,
> Take me to you, imprison me, for I
> Except you enthrall me, never shall be free,
> Nor ever chaste, except you ravish me.

You may think that a sonnet by nature requires a more subdued tone, but Donne's tone is aggressive and passionate. Note his aggressive syntax, the lists of verbs, and the metaphor of a town under siege. God has hold of the speaker's heart, and he "labors to admit" him, but "Oh, to no end." His reason, the speaker explains, is "captived, and proves weak or untrue." But then the tone changes: "Yet dearly I love you." There's sadness wrapped into his passion. His wild contradictions of feeling come across as frustration, love, and endearment—but he also expresses sorrow that he's not able to fully commit himself to God. Still, at the end, he boldly states that he'll never be free or chaste, because God "ravishes" him. The passionate tone of this sonnet is clear.

Ultimate Style

Convey Sadness, Contemplation, or Melancholy

You can use prosaic syntax (sounding more like prose than poetry) and smooth, balanced lines to convey a tone that is sad, contemplative, or melancholy. No matter what sort of form your choose, you can use long, dark, sonorous vowel sounds; cautious, dramatic repetition; and a slow, serious pace to give it a somber quality. Ralph Waldo Emerson masters a melancholy tone in these lines from "Voluntaries":

> Low and mournful be the strain,
> Haughty thought be far from me;
> Tones of penitence and pain,
> Moanings of the tropic sea;

The syntax isn't brisk. Instead of pretty, lyrical *S* sounds and harsh, sharp *B*, *K*, and *T* sounds, Emerson uses many vowel sounds, such as *O*'s: *low, mournful, tones, moanings*. The sonorous sounds draw out your breath and elongate the words, which slows the lines down. These aren't the sounds and rhythms of someone in love; these are the rhythms of someone who seems alone and contemplative, sad and humbled.

Be Ironic

Irony means saying one thing but meaning something else, usually the opposite of what you've said. You can create an ironic tone by using dashes and exclamations, which suggest a possible gap between what is true and what appears to be true. You can also convey irony by using quotation marks, which bring the truth or accuracy of a word or phrase into question: *She said she "loved" me*. By putting *loved* into quotation marks, the speaker is suggesting that she may not have really loved him, even though she said she did. You can also use italics to highlight a word and suggest a possible opposite meaning.

Another way to get at irony is through sarcasm: *Naturally. You're always correct.* Whoever says this most likely means the very opposite. Whenever you see a word such as *every* or *always*, be on the lookout for sarcasm and irony. Finally, you can indicate irony by posing a question or series of questions. By doing so, you can have the speaker of your poem set readers up for an unexpected or surprising answer.

Phillis Wheatley conveys irony in her poem "On Being Brought from Africa to America":

> 'Twas mercy brought me from my pagan land
> Taught my benighted soul to understand
> That there's a God, that there's a Savior too:
> Once I redemption neither sought nor knew.
> Some view our sable race with scornful eye.
> "Their color is a diabolic dye."
> Remember, Christians, Negroes, black as Cain,
> May be refined, and join the angelic train.

Ultimate Style

Wheatley, a black slave, was taught to read and write by her owners, and she eventually became a writer and an activist who fought for the abolition of slavery. With that in mind, we can suspect that it is unlikely that she would actually claim her home was a "pagan land," or that her soul was "benighted." She sarcastically suggests that slave owners taught her about God—but she actually believed slaveholding was incompatible with justice. Was it really "mercy" that brought her to America? It certainly doesn't seem that way. Wheatley uses terms such as *mercy, redemption*, and *angelic* ironically, meaning exactly the opposite of what she says.

Show Joy, Awe, and Love

Long, breathless, run-on sentences and lists are signals that big emotions are at stake. You can write a poem that expresses joy, awe, or love in any form, but the most exuberant poems often share these characteristics. Look how expertly Frank O'Hara uses a breathless sentence and lists in these lines from "Having a Coke With You":

> I look
>
> At you and I would rather look at you than all the portraits in the
>> world
>
> except possibly for the *Polish Rider* occasionally and anyway it's
>> in the Frick
>
> which thank heavens you haven't gone to yet so we can go
>> together for the first time
>
> and the fact you move so beautifully more or less takes care of
>> Futurism

His exuberance goes on to form one long sentence. O'Hara runs through his favorite paintings and happiest feelings about art as a projection and comparison of his love—while understanding that what those paintings lack is the man he's in love with. In other words, his love is what art is all about ("the fact that you move so beautifully more or less takes care of Futurism"). Breathlessly, in one run-on sentence, O'Hara conveys wild emotions, excitement, and hope.

Keep Your Style

You don't have to force an unnatural style just to achieve a certain tone. Tone is part of all poems, no matter what their style, so there's no need to try to write like a poet who, for example, always writes "sad" poems. In these lines from "Kaddish," a long poem about mourning, Allen Ginsberg achieves a tone that is quietly contemplative while still hanging onto his characteristic intensity:

> That's good! That leaves it open for no regret—no fear
>
> radiators, lacklove, torture even toothache in the end—
>
> Though while it comes it is a lion that eats the soul–and the
>
> lamb, the soul, in us, alas, offering itself in sacrifice to
>
> change's fierce hunger—hair and teeth—and the roar of
>
> bonepain, skull bare, break rib, rot-skin, braintricked
>
> Implacability.

Ultimate Style

Throughout the poem, Ginsberg uses long, serene lines and writes in a casual style, as though he's talking to a friend, to convey sadness. At the beginning of the first line shown here, his falsely happy "That's good!" emphasizes sadness and longing: it *would* be nice to think that there would be no regrets and that pain or even a toothache meant nothing in the end. He follows it up with images of a lion eating the soul, or the lamb in us, a subtle reference to religion. What about our hunger, our memories, our pain? Ginsberg is effectively ambiguous, seemingly joyful but not really pleased with the fact of death and the fact that life is what it is, nothing more or less. The tone of the poem is clear, and he achieved it while still staying true to his intense style. He takes poetic techniques and makes them personal.

Tone in Action

In William Wordsworth's "The World Is Too Much with Us," a Petrarchan sonnet, we know one thing from the beginning: there's likely to be a turn, or change in tone, between the initial 8-line octave and the 6-line sestet that follows it. This poem addresses the quality of the modern world, which becomes doubly clear thanks to the tone shift in line 8.

The World Is Too Much with Us

The world is too much with us; late and soon,

Getting and spending, we lay waste our powers;

Little we see in Nature that is ours;

We have given our hearts away, a sordid boon!

This Sea that bares her bosom to the moon,

The winds that will be howling at all hours,

And are up-gathered now like sleeping flowers,

For this, for everything, we are out of tune;

It moves us not.—Great God! I'd rather be

A Pagan suckled in a creed outworn;

So might I, standing on this pleasant lea,

Have glimpses that would make me less forlorn;

Have sight of Proteus rising from the sea;

Or hear old Triton blow his wreathed horn.

In the beginning, Wordsworth's tone is meditative. The first line flows, in iambic pentameter, gracefully. But in line 2, *Getting* is a trochee, not an iamb, and the more aggressive emphasis on that word suggests that whatever it is we are getting is not good. Similarly, the trochee *Little* in line 3 points out bitterly that we see "little" in Nature that's ours anymore. Wordsworth lived in England's rural Lake District, and for him the natural world was not just a walk in the park; it represented the spiritual world. Wordsworth is suggesting that people are missing the point. The workaday material world has led them to overlook the benefits of the natural world.

By line 5, Wordsworth has settled back into a musical iambic pentameter line—the changes in meter reflect the changes in tone. Lines 5, 6, and 7 have a consistent, swaying rhythm. This makes sense: he's talking about Nature, which has a flow, rather than a broken, abbreviated rhythm. The tone has changed from meditative to longing—for the open sea and howling winds.

Now look what happens in line 8, "For this, for everything, we are out of tune." He's providing a musical metaphor: being out of tune stands in for society being out of tune with Nature. "For this, for everything" is iambic pentameter, but as Wordsworth says "we are out of tune" he pulls away from the standard meter and slaps down a few trochees and an extra beat. At this crucial point, between the octave and the sestet, the tone shifts from being concerned to being angry and accusing—we have dismissed Nature. In line 9, again, Wordsworth starts with a few iambs and then throws in a spondee, "Great God!" before using iambs again. The exclamation "Great God" expresses his outrage both in what it says and in the meter it uses.

For the rest of the poem, Wordsworth's tone shifts dramatically. He is so resistant to the modern world that being a Pagan would make him less sad than watching what's happening to the world. In the last two lines, Wordsworth points out how Pagans (the ancient Greeks) had more interest in Nature than we do. After all, they created an entire mythology, assigning gods to aspects of nature, like the sea-god Proteus who could change shapes at will and Triton (Poseidon's son) who liked to blow his (conch shell) horn. Triton blowing his horn underscores the musical metaphor started in line 8. Nature, unlike modern society, is not out of tune, as we see from Triton, who's still blowing his conch-horn.

Ultimate Style

Exercises

- Write a poem in which your tone changes. You can start off in a way that's ironic or aggressive, and soften the tone as you continue—or do it the other way around.

- Write a short, ironic poem about not loving someone—while making it quite clear that you're actually infatuated with him or her.

- Use a series of lists to create a joyful, exuberant poem about your favorite vacation destination. Do the same for your least favorite place—but write the poem as though you love it.

Revision

Getting your poem on paper is an accomplishment you should be proud of—but it's only the first step in creating an excellent poem. Every line and word of a poem needs to be *exactly* right in order for a poem to work, and no poet—unless he or she is very, very lucky—can get a poem right on the first try. Revising your work is one of the most important parts of the writing process.

Revising involves much more than just replacing a word here and there. You need to look at the most fundamental aspects of your poem, including form, line structure, meter, rhyme, and tone. This is the time to make all the components of your poem work together to create a single effect. As you revise, you may find yourself doing more cutting and rewriting than actual changing—and this is fine. Even if you love a word or phrase, don't be afraid to take it out. You can always use it in another poem.

13

Wait and See

The wait-and-see approach to revising is an important part of the process. Once you write the poem and do some preliminary revision work, you should put the poem aside. Do your best to forget about it; work on something new. In a few days, weeks, or months, take out your poem and read it through. Do you still like it? Chances are you'll see plenty of things you can improve, and you'll have a new take on how to fix it up. Distance can help you see your poem more clearly.

Get Specific

A poem is *not* a group of vague, unrelated images or thoughts, and each word and image in your poem needs to be logical and specific. The more specific you can make your poem, the more interesting and effective it will be. When you revise, you should look at all your images and determine how you can improve them. Take a look at this image:

> Helpless dying turtles reenter the water
> and leave their shells on the beach.

This image doesn't give us enough information. We see two adjectives, *helpless* and *dying*, but these aren't very vivid. Images involve much more than adjectives—they involve constructing a vivid scene. As you edit, add details. You need to say more than just "turtles reenter the water": you should stop and think about why you're talking about the turtles and what's interesting about them. *Why* are the turtles here? Elizabeth Bishop creates a vivid image with these turtles in "Florida":

> Enormous turtles, helpless and mild,
> die and leave their barnacled shells on the beaches,
> and their large white skulls with round eye-sockets
> twice the size of man's.

We see the enormous turtles dying on the beach, their shells crusted with barnacles, and their "large white skulls" with "round eye-sockets." Comparing the turtles' skulls with a man's skull also suggests that more is being described here than simply turtles on a beach. She creates a successful image.

By improving your images, you'll create a story of sorts, with concrete things for the reader to think about. As you revise, go through the lines one by one and consider how the images can be improved. Don't say "tree," say "towering oak"; don't say "flower," say "soft-fringed orchid petals"; and don't say "winter," say "ice-lashed streets." Soon you'll find yourself with a much meatier poem than the one you began with.

Use Verbs Carefully

Active verbs can give your poem movement and excitement, but make sure you haven't overdone it. Take a look at these three lines, in which the verbs are bolded:

> The sun **shines** brightly on the turf,
> where the cold wind **blows**. Leaves
> **litter** the field where he **marches**.

There are too many verbs, too close together. Instead of being able to clearly imagine what's happening in your poem, readers will be overwhelmed—the overabundance of verbs blurs the focus of the poem. To improve these lines, decide what action is the most important, and revise your poem to focus on that. You can also take straightforward lines such as these and rework them so that they have more impact. Here's a better version:

> Sun on the turf, where cold wind **blows**,
> and his footsteps over leaves littering the field.

The first version sounds like prose and is too balanced. There's no driving action because so many verbs are scattered around the lines. Also, too many little words clutter up the lines. In the revision, we have only one active verb (*blows*), and the poem turns on that word alone. "Sun on the turf" is far more rhythmic and elegant than the predictable Dick-and-Jane version, "The sun shines brightly on the turf." We've gone from three lines to two lines, and we have a much tighter, more effective poem.

Question Form

If you're writing a poem in form, you should question why you chose to do so. If you were writing in a form as an exercise or a challenge, that's fine—but now that you have a poem in front of you, you should make it as good as it can be even if that means changing the form. Using form for form's sake doesn't make for an effective poem, since the form serves no true purpose. Your poem has to sound good as a *poem*, not as a poem in form.

Just because you've written a poem that meets all the requirements of a form such as a villanelle or a sonnet doesn't mean your poem is finished. Think of the finished product as a first draft. Read it out loud. If the poem sounds stilted or stiff, or if it lacks rhythm, the form isn't working. Form should enhance the rhythm, not detract from it. If the lines sound unrelated to each other, or if they make no sense, you need to revise them, no matter how much you wind up unraveling the form. Now look at the diction. Have you shoved certain words into place because they fit the form? Is each word *exactly* the word you needed?

Go from word to word, line to line, until you're completely satisfied with every detail. Don't hesitate to add words or phrases even if they don't fit in the form. The sentences and the sense of the poem are more important than the form.

Loosen Up Meter

If you're writing a poem in meter, it's essential not to consider it a finished product until the meter is *good*—versus just *done*. Anyone can write a poem in meter, but too often poets just fill out the meter, rather than enliven it. Here's an example of filling out the meter:

> The Ozarks, full of mountains, meadows, birds
> Dissolve, in winter weather, to a sheet
> Of ice, with towering, snowcapped conifers

This is pretty dull and descriptive. The iambic pentameter is just plodding along, doing nothing exciting and saying nothing that's not plainly descriptive—and even the description isn't exciting. When you revise, make sure the effectiveness of your poem hasn't been sacrificed for the sake of maintaining perfect meter. Loosen it up to let your poem breathe. It's better to work the meter around what you have to say, rather than working what you say around a preestablished pattern. To revise, read the lines out loud, as though they're not written in meter. Revise according to what you want to say—*then* touch up the meter. If it can't be retouched without wrecking the new idea or rhythm, don't force it. Take a look at how we can revise the three dull lines:

> Foliage of Ozarks: currant-purple
> In fall, the swell of hills, bird-calls at day-
> Break linger even after roads dissolve,
> in winter's ice claws, snow-capped conifers.

Ultimate Style

The first line, previously in iambic pentameter, is now trochaic pentameter, five feet of accented and then unaccented syllables. The second line is all iambic pentameter, except the fourth foot—*bird-calls*—which is a trochee. The third line starts with a spondee as a substitution and then slides into iambic pentameter. Finally, line 4, also iambic pentameter, includes two spondee substitutions: "ice claws," "snow-capped." All these substitutions add rhythm and sharpness to the lines. They begin suddenly, dramatically, with the word *foliage* instead of *the*. The zippy, concise, and image-rich first line is then slowed by the iambic rhythms of the second. The surprisingly enjambed "day-break," split over two lines, forces you forward and into another spondee, pausing interestingly on the word *linger*. And instead of just racing through the last line, you slow down again over the two spondees in the middle, both conjunctions and terms that engage two different senses—touch and sight. Loosening up meter has made these lines come alive.

Scrutinize Rhymes

When you revise, you should look closely at your rhymes to make sure they're serving your poem well. Are the rhymes interesting? Do you have a mix of slant rhymes, pure rhymes, and rhymes that involve words of more than one syllable? If every rhyme is something like *true/blue*, you should go back and try to make your rhymes more varied. Consider making simplistic rhymes more sophisticated, such as *true/tray* or *true/tree*. Varying rhymes this way shows you're attentive to the sounds in your poem, a mark of an expert.

To help improve your rhymes, flip through a rhyming dictionary and look at lists of rhymes. You may find a better rhyme, but, more important, you'll spark your creative process by facing so many options. When you look at potential rhymes and consider how they might work in your poem, you'll be forced to think about what you're actually trying to say. You might find that reconsidering a rhyme makes you reconsider an entire line. Rhymes should make sense in context, and you shouldn't include rhymes simply because they fit. Cheap, purposeless rhymes can ruin a poem and alienate your readers. If a rhyme isn't working, or if it calls attention to itself, delete it.

Here's an example of a rhyme that fits its context:

> Along this boardwalk, among the Russian language clear
> and soft as fine vodka, twisted Yiddish has disappeared
> into slang

Clear and *disappeared* are linked by assonance more than rhyme, but they work because the second word doesn't bring you in a different direction entirely. It's related in meaning and linked by the rhyme. Here's the same example with a different rhyme that seems forced:

> Along this boardwalk, among the Russian language clear
> and soft as fine vodka, young boys drinking a beer
> at noon

Why *beer*? Why go to all that length to talk about the Russian language and then mention that some boys are drinking beer? It seems like that was just the easiest rhyme to slip in, without thinking. When you revise, you should be on the lookout for easy rhymes that don't seem vital to your poem.

Intensify Rhythm

Revising rhythm is the most difficult part of revising a poem, because rhythm includes everything that goes into a poem. Think about what rhythm means: the ebb and flow of the sea, trees rustling in autumn, wild snow flurries, a brisk walk. Now think about changes in those rhythms: the pulling back of low tide, trees quiet or suddenly raging in a storm, snow letting up, a racing walk or a slowing down. Now try to think about combining those: the breeze shakes the leaves in the trees, then dies down and there's silence, then builds up into a storm, with terrible noise and rustling. That's what your poem should sound like.

Rhythm isn't a matter of a redundant, metronomic beat. Rhythm is the *change* in that beat. And whether you're writing in meter or free verse, rhythm is equally important and can be equally evasive. Rhythm can make or break a poem. To revise rhythm, look carefully at the following elements in your poem:

- **Line length:** Make sure your lines aren't so long that you get bogged down in them, and not so short you don't have time to take them in. If every line is the same length, try varying them. If every line has the same sentence structure, change them around for more variety.

- **Sounds:** Make sure you're using a balanced blend of pure rhymes, slant rhymes, and similar sounds, and that you're not overdoing it. If every line is rhymed and also matches up with three rhymes inside that line, you've probably gone overboard.

- **Pacing:** The lines and sentences should move at different speeds—some fast, some slow, some very slow.

- **Meter:** You should mark out the meter by scanning the poem and looking for places where you could use substitutions to vary the rhythm.

- **Repetition:** If you've used repetition, make sure it sounds musical and not careless. If you haven't used repetition, consider adding some to intensify the rhythm.

- **Diction:** Make sure your words aren't all one syllable (unless you're going for a particular effect) or that there aren't too many long words piled up together.

With all this in mind, you should look closely at each and every line and consider how all these elements work together to create rhythm. Are there pauses in the sentences, and forcefully enjambed lines, followed by, say, a spondee? Should an end-stopped line be enjambed? Is the diction varied and accurate? Take a look at this line:

Ultimate Style

> Knotted rememberings, occasional horsefly gnawings punctuating the countryside

There are far too many long words, and they drown the rhythm. But be careful not to veer too far in the opposite direction:

> Twice, blue found objects swim far

It sounds like you're reading from a menu. Vary the diction and length of the syllables:

> Twice, blue found-objects, underwater, swam farther

That's already better. Now there are three caesuras, not one, a conjunction (*found-objects*), a four-syllable word, and the assonance and multisyllable effect of "swam farther." That line has rhythm. Looking at each of your own lines and breaking them down word by word will help you improve the rhythm of your own poem.

Check the Logic

You can line edit, fix up your verbs, and spruce up your diction and syntax. But does it make sense? Your poem needs to have some kind of logic. That doesn't mean your poem has to be obvious or simple; poetry is often ambiguous. But you, at least, should know exactly what you're saying in the poem, even if it's not explicit. You can write from the gut, but when you revise, you'll need to see if it makes sense. You may have to add a few images, lines, or even stanzas to give the logic of your poem more traction.

Improve Your Title

The title is the first thing people see if your poem is printed in a journal or a book. If your poem has a boring title, you may lose potential readers who will decide to read something that sounds more exciting. The title is also the first thing listeners hear at a poetry reading, and it's often what sticks. You should think carefully about your title—spend plenty of time on it. Think about it while you're writing the poem and when you revise it.

Perhaps you'll find a phrase in your poem that works as a title. Or perhaps you just want to make the title a straightforward summing up of the poem. Regardless, it's a good idea to think about the title when you put the draft of your poem aside for a few weeks. When you come back to it, you'll probably have a better idea whether the title you picked is working, or, if you haven't chosen a title, what a good title might be.

When choosing a title, put yourself into your readers' shoes. Ask yourself the following questions:

- Does the title make you want to read further?
- Does it suggest something weird or odd that piques your interest?
- Does it *feel* right to you? In other words, does it "match" the poem?

Sparking Curiosity   A good title intrigues readers. Some titles do sum up their poems, but if you decide your poem is about hope and you call your poem "Hope," you won't intrigue anyone. Titles such as "Love," "Pain," and "Sadness" don't really tell people anything about your poem—instead, they suggest you just couldn't think of a better title. An intriguing title stands out and makes you want to read the poem. Take a look at the following titles:

"Frostbite on Denali"
"Mistake"
"Exclaims the River"
"Hope and Light"
"Sunset at Mount Penobscot"
"Ode to My Dog"
"The Sea"
"Ocean of Green Walnuts"

Everyone has different reactions to titles, but here are some thoughts:

- "Frostbite on Denali" seems somewhat compelling, as though there's a story there about climbing an icy, cold mountain.
- "Mistake" and "Hope and Light" are too simple and too vague. They don't say anything new or interesting.
- "Exclaims the River" is attention-grabbing: it starts with an active verb, *exclaims*, and raises the question of what, exactly, the river is exclaiming—especially since rivers don't talk.
- "Sunset on Mount Penobscot," is decent, but not great. It lacks uniqueness.
- "Ode to My Dog" intrigues because it's humorous.
- "The Sea"—what about the sea? It doesn't suggest anything special.
- "Ocean of Green Walnuts" is an excellent title. It creates a peculiar image: an ocean of green, unripe walnuts. Naturally, this ocean doesn't exist, but it's the kind of title that compels you to read on.

Learning from the Masters   Some poets, such as T. S. Eliot, are masters of titles, and others, such as Yeats, are not. Here's a sampling by Eliot:

"The Love Song of J. Alfred Prufrock"
"Burbank with a Baedeker: Bleistein with a Cigar"
"A Cooking Egg"

Part of the excitement is in the sounds. These lines all have abrupt, sharp sounds. Would we be as interested in a love song by David Smith? Probably not. Prufrock sounds sillier, and he doesn't sound like someone likely to sing a love song. The second title, packed with *B* sounds, is clumsy and blundering, and so it stands out. "A Cooking Egg" is so ordinary it seems ridiculous—but you want to find out what he possibly has to say about an egg that's cooking. The words themselves don't have to be exciting or odd, but they do need to make an impact, whether it's through the sound of the title or the potential meaning that's being conveyed.

Ultimate Style

Here are some dull titles by Yeats:

"The Lover's Song"
"A Prayer for Old Age"
"Those Images"
"Statistics"

Yeats was a master poet, but his titles aren't always electrifying. They're generally simple, and, like "The Lover's Song," aren't especially captivating. However, keep in mind that simple titles are fine if you avoid clichés and if you choose your words thoughtfully. The titles of two excellent poems by Philip Larkin, "Water" and "Church Going," are effective because they're straightforward without being sappy.

Revision in Action

When you revise a poem, you may make small changes, such as selecting a different word here and there or breaking a line slightly differently, or you may scrap your original poem and start from scratch, keeping only a phrase or an idea or two. Take a look at this before-and-after example from Diane Mehta:

First Draft

The rain-triggered sweat of half-dry, reddening leaves

paused. The annual, child-hearted passions: icicles sharp as
     wonder,

muscle-nourishing milk, and apples chewed whole, around the
     skin.

A racket, Sunday sparrows on the facades of limestone.

The fluttering, shadow songs of monosyllables

in a child's voice.

The coarse dusk as if

the sky flipped inside out—

the gates of every home at ease

like tropical, lazy waterfalls

and the moon faintly preaches;

this could be you or while the syncopated

onslaught of black frost,

a 22 karat moon that pretends to be noon,

magnetism and the planet's angle.

This could be, worse, true.

Sign the book. The tree is gathering
dust and dusk but is still alive
while ironwork and alarms all up the block
Burn out the fear. Later, winter
cuts in like scissors, silver, spearing.

Revision
Rain-sweat of half-dry, reddening leaves.
A prayer-exempt year.
Sky, between mirrors, flipped inside out,

**Ultimate
Style**

its ruffled, uplifted colors
fluttering, like shadow-clatter of sparrows,
down, cinematic-style, all at once

the way Cezanne must have seen it: thickly clear,
gold-fringed, as if the mind knew better.
A sunburst in fronds, tinged with the blood of winter.

Embedded in my eyes are 19 months my son
has been alive, with *blue* slang for crayons,
spoons and fly swatters shovels

in his eyes. 19 months etched upon my face
stonework inscriptions, rust-glaze of seasons
curving, dark frost and love-light photosynthesis.

But the year is turning, my skin,
fire-bound, unlearning its natural inclinations.
The interior excitement flies sideways

without the enlivening sun-after
sundown makes believe comes later.
A prayer-exempt year of half-words

shaping months into the music of sentences
complete as the mind grasps, its tiny fingers
pointing at everything it sees.

Commentary   First drafts are just a starting point, a place
in which you put down everything and anything you think
about, whether it makes sense or not. Look closely at the first
draft of this poem, then at the revised version. They're vastly
different poems. Instead of two stanzas, the revision is divided
into eight stanzas of three lines each—a tighter, more even
form. Whereas in the original, the lines were of vastly different lengths, the line length is more regular in the revision.
The imagery, rhythm, and music of the revision are all much
stronger than those of the original version.

Not *everything* has changed, however. The revision
contains a few phrases from the original, such as "Rain-sweat
of half-dry, reddening leaves." This resembles the original, but
it's tighter, with fewer words and a more concise, vivid image. A
few lines later in the revision, "flipped inside out" appears, also
a holdover from the first draft. Besides these phrases, you can
also see ghosts of ideas from the first draft. But all the first draft
did was *hint* at what would eventually be clear in the revision—the physical scene, the seasons changing, the idea that
as the child grows death gets closer for the parent. The revision
has crystallized those ideas and presented them in a skillful,
lovely way.

Exercises

- Find a poem you really dislike and edit it into a poem you can call your own. This will force you to really concentrate, line by line, on what should be cut and why it was put there in the first place.

- Write a poem about anything in five minutes. Edit for another five minutes, then throw that version away. Now write the same poem again, this time taking as long as you need to work through it and edit carefully. This should help you stay attached to your thoughts and ideas, not the poem.

Ultimate Style

- Find a poem you love and edit it down to five lines. This exercise will force you to cut phrases you're attached to—an important part of editing, especially when interesting lines aren't working in a particular poem—and to remain concise.

Writing Workshops

Showing your poems to others is an important part of the writing and learning process. When you work on a poem for a long time, you lose the ability to see it objectively: you're so familiar with it that you're incapable of recognizing weaknesses or problems. Other people, however, have never seen your poem before—they can look at it with fresh eyes and point out things that you may have never seen on your own.

Getting feedback on your work makes your poems better—but workshops can help your writing in another way too. By reading other people's work closely and making thoughtful comments, you'll gain a deeper understanding of poetry in general. You'll be more finely attuned to how poetic elements work in real poems, and you'll be able to apply what you learn to your own writing.

14

Set Up an Effective Workshop

The most important aspect of a writing workshop is that it gives you critical feedback to help you improve your poems, and, over the years, professional and student writers have come to a few conclusions about what makes a workshop effective. You should consider these elements when you're thinking about starting your own workshop.

Location Location sets the workshop's tone and atmosphere. If you meet somewhere crowded and busy, noise and people-watching will be distracting. However, sterile environments (the library, an empty classroom) feel so dreary and official that the workshop may become a drag. The best locations provide a perfect combination of comfort, quiet, and convenience. Consider a local coffee shop during off-peak hours, a friend's house, or a park. All of these locations allow you to enjoy your environment while still encouraging focus.

Size The optimal size for a workshop is four to six people. Fewer than four people isn't recommended: there will invariably be a meeting when two people can't make it. If you have more than six people, all sorts of potential issues arise: not being able to find a large enough location, mini-discussions breaking out during a critique, insufficient time for everyone to present work, and comments so diverse that incorporating them into your work is impossible.

Ultimate Style

Participants Don't invite just anyone to your workshop. It's a place for people who are serious about writing and who are looking for constructive feedback. You can ask poetry-writing friends or classmates to join, as well as seek out participants from message boards, school poetry clubs, or poetry programs at colleges and universities. When you talk to potential members, ask why they want to join and what they think they can get out of the workshop. It doesn't matter who's published or who's better—what really matters is who's a good critic and who knows how to be critical without being harsh.

Follow a Schedule

The best way to maintain order in a group of emotional people eager to talk about their poems is to follow a schedule. Try to meet once a week for a reasonable amount of time. An optimal duration is one that allows every participant to have a turn without feeling short-changed by the dwindling attention of those who get bored easily. Ultimately, you'll have to determine the duration of your workshop according to the number of participants, but a good rule of thumb is that two and a half hours is the maximum time you can expect people to stay focused.

Set a specific limit on the time each participant's work is discussed. Failing to do so will result in certain participants taking up too much time with endless questions and others stuck with only five minutes of feedback. A reasonable length for each person is twenty to thirty minutes. Each session should begin with one member of the workshop—not the poet whose work is being discussed—reading the poem in question out loud.

Be Prepared

Make sure that everyone's work is sent out to all the participants before your workshop meets. Reading work during meetings is a waste of time, and participants won't have time to consider their feedback carefully. It's also a good idea to ask all the participants to print out the poems and write their comments on the pages. This way, you'll receive feedback from everyone, not just the most talkative participants.

Give Constructive Feedback

Constructive criticism is feedback that focuses on potential solutions rather than problems. This is more than just polite: it's the best way to help people to understand how to progress and make changes. You should never make fun of someone's poem or writing style, and you shouldn't spend the entire time pointing out all the problems in someone's poem. Constructive criticism is a way of *helping* someone by pointing out possible flaws and offering suggestions on how to make the poem better.

Ultimate Style

Helpful Hints   Here are a few helpful hints for providing constructive criticism:

- Ask questions: "I'm not sure if I'm reading this correctly, but is the speaker of the poem saying that all love is ambiguous?"

- Refer to the "speaker" of the poem, not the poet, when asking questions about the meaning or content. The poet is not necessarily the speaker of the poem, and during a workshop you should *always* treat the two as separate entities.

- Deliver both criticism and praise. There's usually something redeeming about a poem, so say so: "I think the poem doesn't work in this form because it feels too heavy, especially for such a light subject. But I like the imagery, especially the phrases about oranges."

- Provide at least one potential solution for each problem. If you can think of more, suggest them all.

- Always let the poet know that your suggestions are only your opinions. You can begin your sentences with "I think" or "Here's one possibility I thought of." This softens the blow that would be felt if you instead said, "You don't" or "Your problem is …"

- Don't try to convince someone that your solution is the only way to go. You may feel you're right, but remember that not everyone sees things the same way. Your job isn't to write someone else's poem—it's to provide them with other options and opinions.

Constructive Praise   Everyone likes to hear nice things about their work, but praising a poem to the skies during a workshop is unhelpful. It's fine to compliment the poet and point out things you love, but don't let this be the only type of comment you make. People are in the workshop to *work* on their poems—respect that. If you like something, be specific: "I really like the wit and turns of phrase, especially when they're done with the rhymes at the end of the line." You can also compare the things you like to other poems you've seen by the same poet: "The style you've been writing in seems to really suit you—it's snappy, with lots of quirky rhymes and abrupt phrases."

Learn to Read Others' Work

To read other people's work critically, you need to use a different set of skills than you use when you read for pleasure. Instead of trying to grasp the meaning of a poem or simply enjoy the language, you need to analyze every word in every stanza for effectiveness. You're trying to identify weaknesses and come up with suggestions for improvement. The first key to reading critically is to focus on one or two elements each time you read through a poem. Reading the same work several times will increase your understanding and help you to give better feedback. It goes without saying that you shouldn't read that week's poems ten minutes before the workshop begins: you should put the same amount of effort into critiquing others' work as you put into writing your own.

What to Look For   To give thorough, detailed feedback, you need to look at various poetic elements. Ask yourself the following questions to get started with your critique:

- What's in the title? Does it give you a clue as to the poem's meaning?

- What kind of images are used in the poem? What do they mean? Does the poem need more or better images?

- Do the similes and metaphors work? Do they make sense in context?

- What is the form, if there is one? Is meter used? Does the form contribute to or support the poem in some way, or is it irrelevant? What would be the best form for that poem?

- If the poem is in form, would it work better as free verse?

- Are line breaks effective? Does each line break seem right? They *all* need to work, so if one seems forced, point it out.

- Are the rhymes obvious and simplistic, or are they interesting or surprising?

- What's the tone of the poem? How is tone conveyed? Is the poem full of abrupt stops; harsh, cacophonous sounds; or jazz-like beats? Is the language lyrical and soft?

- What happens during the poem? Think about the events of the poem, even if they seem minor or unimportant.

- What does the poem have too much of and what does it have too little of? Focus on imagery, rhythm, sounds, diction, and metaphors.

- Does the poem seem haphazardly written? Could you substitute a word for another and not know the difference?

- Does the poem have rhythm? Is the rhythm lacking or stilted, or is it jazzy, smart, and graceful? Does the rhythm have drama, or does it feel flat?

- What do you feel when you read the poem?

Decipher the Poem

You have a poem in front of you from someone in your workshop, and you just don't get it. Don't worry: you don't have to get it. Instead of searching for the full meaning, search for clues. What kinds of words are used? What do the sounds convey? Is the poem full of harsh sounds and abrupt pauses or smoothly flowing lines? Diction and syntax will give you a hint about the tone, which will help you figure out what the poem is about.

A poem doesn't have to be about something concrete. Make a list of all the abstract concepts in the poem and see if a theme or connection appears. If you still can't get it, don't worry. Others probably won't get it either. You can point this out in your constructive criticism: "I like the imagery, but I don't really get it. It might help to have some clues about the meaning, even in the title."

Ultimate Style

Accept Feedback Gracefully

If you think reading others' work critically and providing constructive criticism is hard, wait until you're in the hot seat. Receiving comments on your work can be difficult for three main reasons:

- It's hard to keep up with everyone's comments, especially when they contradict one another.
- You have to think quickly to process the information you're given and figure out if it works or not.

- You have to deal with people tearing apart your precious writing—people who may have never heard of constructive criticism.

The key to receiving feedback is to be organized. You should bring a copy of your poem and a notebook to the workshop. Try to write down every note you get, as you'll find that you've forgotten half of them by the next day. If a comment doesn't make sense, ask for clarification. Don't worry about seeming dense or stubborn—someone might have a great solution for you, but it's useless if you can't understand it.

Even though you should feel free to ask people exactly what they mean, you shouldn't argue with people who are volunteering constructive criticism. It's common to get feedback that you just don't agree with, but keep it to yourself. You may find yourself tempted to say "What I meant was ..." However, if the group is telling you that whatever you meant to say didn't come across, take that to heart. If everyone's saying the same thing, you might consider listening.

Keeping Perspective   Remember: a workshop isn't there to write the poem for you. In the end, it's your poem. Think about what others have said, and think about your strengths and weaknesses in general. If you're sure about something, but no one else is, there's nothing wrong with doing it your way.

A Final Note

Learning to write an excellent poem is an ongoing process. Every poem you write will be different—each will begin from a different spark of an idea, and each may take an entirely different form. Each time you sit down and begin to write, you'll have to start from the very beginning. However, understanding the basic elements of writing poetry will help take the mystery out of writing—you'll know exactly what to do, every step of the way.

Like anything else, practice makes perfect. As you write, you'll discover your own writing style and your own best strategies for creating a poem. You'll work out the kinks and see how all the techniques work together to help you write an excellent poem, every time.

Don't let that blank page or computer screen scare you off! Now you know what to do, so you can get started. Good luck!

Permission Credits

Grateful acknowledgment is given for permission to reprint these poems. Every effort has been made to seek the appropriate permission to reprint poems and excerpts of poems.

"Pantoum," from SOME TREES, by John Ashbery. Copyright © 1956 by John Ashbery. Reprinted by permission of Georges Borchardt, Inc., on behalf of the author.

"Funeral Blues," copyright © 1940 and renewed 1968 by W.H. Auden, from COLLECTED POEMS by W.H. Auden. Used by permission of Random House, Inc.

Excerpts from "At the Fishhouses" and "Florida" and "The Fish" from THE COMPLETE POEMS 1927-1979 by Elizabeth Bishop. Copyright © 1979, 1983 by Alice Helen Methfessel. Reprinted by permission of Farrar, Straus and Giroux, LLC.

"In the Same Space" from THE COMPLETE POEMS OF CAVAFY, copyright © 1961 and renewed 1989 by Rae Dalven, reprinted by permission of Harcourt, Inc. This material may not be reproduced in any form or by any means without the prior written permission of the publisher.

"An hour is a sea," reprinted by permission of the publishers and the Trustees of Amherst College from THE POEMS OF

About the Author

Diane Mehta is a New York–based poet and critic. Her poems have appeared in *Poetry, Southern Review, Gettysburg Review, Witness, Bomb, Western Humanities Review, Flaneur, Notre Dame Review, Harvard Review, Open City, Callaloo, Literary Review, Antioch Review,* and several anthologies of Indian American writing. Her book reviews and essays have appeared in the *Atlantic Monthly* and many other literary magazines. In 1993, she was a poetry fellow in Boston University's graduate writing program.